MW01094039

the
SOLITARY
CEO

How to Overcome the Isolation
That's Holding You Back

PATRICK SALLEE

FREILING
PUBLISHING

Published by Freiling Publishing,
a division of Freiling Agency, LLC.

P.O. Box 1264
Warrenton, VA 20188

www.FreilingPublishing.com

HB ISBN: 978-1-956267-75-4
eBook ISBN: 978-1-956267-76-1

Printed in the United States of America

Contents

"We are all broken by something. We have all hurt someone and have been hurt. We all share the condition of brokenness even if our brokenness is not equivalent."

—*Bryan Stevenson*

I've spent my entire career working in the nonprofit sector, focused on organizations that work in under-resourced communities, with the intent of impacting change on a broad scale that can impact people's lives. People don't get into this line of work for the money or the glory; it is about the impact.

A quote at the end of a motion picture called *The Guilty* says, "Broken people save broken people." While I'm not skilled enough to really save lives, this statement of impact succinctly covers my "why."

My career has afforded me the opportunity to meet some amazing people from all backgrounds and walks of life. The intersection at many organizations between the people in need, those that help provide services/programs, and the generous donors that make it possible is a fascinating connection. I'm thoroughly convinced that we have a path forward that can change how services are provided by thinking about how we leverage community-centered investments to reduce poverty, improve health, and advance racial equity.

When I was arrested, I was lucky enough to work for an amazing boss who gave me the time and space to do what I needed to do so I could get my life in order and begin walking down a path of sobriety. The arrest and subsequent jail time had little impact on my career at the time. It was a huge privilege to work for two people who accepted me even with my background and trusted that I could still perform the job they needed. I'm incredibly lucky to have been given those chances.

I also want to pause here a moment to comment on privilege. I am a straight, white, male and I understand the privilege that brings to many of the personal circumstances I describe in this book. I recognize that the grace and opportunity I've been given to pursue different roles and leadership would face different challenges if I looked different than I do. It is that difference, and the experiences I've had, that motivate me to work in the industry and organization I do and how I try to show up and create space every day.

———— ❧ ————

While there is a lot in this book about lessons learned in recovery and my individual experience, there isn't much direct advice or input on alcoholism and addiction. There are a couple of reasons for this. First, I'm not an expert. I have one experience with sobriety and know what has worked for me. I would never claim that my approach would work for everyone; it has just been my experience. Second, the goal of this book isn't to serve as a primer on recovery, but it is my personal take on how some behaviors have worked well in approaching leadership roles.

Additionally, if you or someone you know is struggling with addiction, some resources have been provided below for support and assistance: https://www.hazeldenbettyford.org/about-us/news-media/coronavirus-disease-response/free-recovery-resources

Introduction

"You may not realize it when it happens, but a kick in the teeth may be the best thing in the world for you."

—Walt Disney

I stared at a black-and-white striped jumpsuit and my unshaven face in a rusty jail cell mirror.

Knowing my actions put me in that place forced me to re-evaluate my life, my choices, and what I was going to do next. It is a mental image I will never forget, because I never want to see it again.

It would have been easy to convince myself, "This isn't me; I don't belong here." But that would have been another lie. I would have been lying to myself. And the only choice I had was to stop—stop convincing myself I didn't have a problem, and stop covering up the partying and the bad choices. I had only one choice, and that was to work to turn my life around.

At the time, I had no way of knowing what life would look like in the future. All I knew was that it couldn't continue down the same path. As I look back now, I don't recognize the person I was. I know I made poor choices, but that person is different on the inside now.

There was nothing more humbling than a conversation around a jail lunch table. Nobody cared about where I was from, what I did for a living, or how special I thought I was. My life was never the topic of discussion, and nobody would be impressed even if it were. At best, I would get: "What the hell are you doing here?" In jail, everything was stripped away. The things I used to define myself disappeared—my job, my status, and my education. Since all the people around me were on equal footing, none of that mattered. Jail is the ultimate equalizer, and in that way, it is the ultimate belittler. But jail, and particularly solitary confinement, is where this book begins. It's also how I learned lifelong lessons that made me a better person, and consequently, a more engaged, effective, and balanced leader.

Since you're reading this book, I'm going to assume that you feel "lonely at the top." You're probably a little—or maybe a lot—weary of the daily leadership grind. You want to become a better leader, but you're also fatigued, even exasperated, and you have a hard time finding the help you need to lead with more balance and engagement. You might have resorted to some self-destructive habits that eventually, when outed, will destroy what you've worked so hard for. You might even be a lot closer than you realize to "cracking," and I assume you're reading this book because you intuitively know it.

How do I know this? Because it is lonely at the top. Like most clichés, it is a cliché because it is true. But the difference, which I started to appreciate when I spent a lot of time alone in a jail cell, is that it doesn't have to always be true.

Several lessons throughout this book I learned the hard way, and there are many commonalities. Often leadership is all about the leader. I will attempt to make the case that the opposite is true: Leadership is about everyone else. It is counterintuitive to the things that often get us into leadership roles, but it's true. Life in a leadership role doesn't have to be lonely and frustrating; it can be immensely fulfilling and rewarding work. It can be an opportunity to improve the lives of all the people around you with greater fulfillment and rewards, which ultimately causes organizations to grow stronger and healthier.

We see all around us how CEOs and other leaders privately and then very publicly slip into self-destructive habits that bring them down, and sometimes their entire organizations with them. Seldom a day goes by when we don't read about a business leader, a politician, a non-profit executive, or even a minister who made a series of terrible moral or ethical decisions that, when made public, seemed shockingly sudden. But they aren't sudden at all. The slippery slope of bad decisions can be insidiously slow. One bad decision creeps into another, and then another. Soon everything around us collapses, and we wonder how it all started. The fact is that it started in private, on the inside. That's what happened to me before I found myself in solitary confinement.

Writing this book has been on my mind for a long time. I have felt that the lessons I've learned can help others with their leadership challenges and how they view their roles with a more open and engaging approach. The first thing I want you to know is that you aren't alone. I have discovered that leadership can indeed be a lonely place, but much of it was my own making. I had become my own worst enemy. My message to you is that you likely feel alone because you've boxed yourself in. You've constructed and walked into your own lonely, private cell, and then you slammed the door. You've become a self-fulfilling prophecy. I'm here to help you discover how to get out of your cell, to enter life again, and to engage with yourself and your organization so you will be healthier mentally, emotionally, and even physically. That's what this book is about. I want to help you feel that you've got a boardroom full of friends at the top, people who want to share in your mission, your vision, your work, and even your life. You will no longer be alone in a cell, but you will be free to be the leader you were meant to be.

I try to learn something new each day, no matter how small. In the last ten years, since I took my last drink of alcohol, the world has taught me a lot.

Today I serve as the CEO of a fast-growing public health organization in Kansas City. We are a social justice and equity organization, operating through the lens of health care. We provide access to medical, dental, and behavioral health services to nearly twenty thousand patients. As we build and grow our organization, I often think back to a time in my life that I'm not proud of but am grateful for, as it helped me become the person I am today. I'm a long way from my jail cell and even further away from feeling lonely at the top.

What do I know about a jail cell?

Before we jump into this book together, let me tell you a little more about my story. As I was building my career through strong performance and great job opportunities, my personal and professional life cascaded into a series of dreadful mistakes and bad choices. On the outside, I was proud of who I was and what I'd become, especially in such short order (I was still in my early thirties). But inside, I was crashing and had resorted to alcohol and other bad habits. The stress of my work got to me, and unfortunately, also to all the people around me, including my family. To make a long story short, due to multiple DUI convictions, I had to spend weeks in jail. While recognizing this isn't months or years, one thing I learned quickly was that any time spent in jail required a significant mental adjustment. It was as if I entered an entirely different world.

When I was initially arrested, I was in a holding place until my court date. It was a group of cells surrounding a common area that all my jail mates had access to at meal times and for another hour or so per day. I had the (relative) freedom to go in and out of my single cell at various times. There were times when I would be alone in my cell to read and think. But I also had opportunities for some interaction with other people. It was certainly not what I had hoped for in my life, but it was bearable, and it gave me the opportunity to begin to recalibrate my life. The environment was tolerable, and it felt more or less safe.

After my court date and sentencing, I was sent to a county jail. I found the situation to be very different when I was herded into a large room with a larger group of inmates. The room was divided into smaller sections of pods with bunk beds and one single (very) public toilet and sink. We spent most of the day in the large group area with opportunities for all sorts of interactions with other people. I'm not in general a people person, but I definitely wasn't there to make friends. As they played cards, posturing and evaluating the "newbies," my anxiety increased, so I asked my attorney about alternatives. He told me, "If you really want to be alone, you could always ask for solitary." My initial thought, which later proved to be a profound miscalculation, was that solitary confinement sounded quite manageable for one week. Little did I know the anxiety that drove that decision would soon be overwhelmed by the solitude.

Shortly after my request, a guard came to get me. As we walked the long and very wide hallway to a different section of the jail, he asked me, "Are you sure you want to do this?"

The way he asked me the question was a bit worrying. "Yeah," I replied, "I'm not here that long, and I want peace and quiet."

I don't think he believed me. But I tried to convince myself this would be a week to unplug, reflect, and sleep. Knowing it wasn't a long time, I tried to convince myself to make the most of it. It's comical now to think about it.

The walk with the guard seemed to take forever. It started to feel more like a dungeon than a prison. We finally reached a heavy steel door leading to a hallway of individual cells. The door slammed shut, and the guard let me choose a few books from a common area. Then he escorted me into my concrete cell that was half the size of my daughter's nursery. I entered, and the guard locked the door shut. It was a jarring feeling to look at a door without a lock on the inside. I was completely at the mercy of everyone on the outside. I sat on my metal bed with a one-inch-thick mattress and pancake-thin pillow, a toilet, a sink, and a mirror.

I looked around at the concrete, which was all painted a very bright white, and then the single light bulb, which never turned off, 24/7. I was locked in my small cell twenty-three hours a day with zero interaction with anyone. At one point, I asked the guards what time it was, and their response was "You don't need to know."

So all I could do was to sit there utterly alone with my thoughts. I'm not the most extroverted or social person by any stretch, but other than the guard who slipped my meal through a small window into my cell, I didn't see or talk to anyone. I don't just mean I wasn't able to talk to people—I mean I literally did not see or talk to anyone else. It didn't take long for the small cell to close in on me. I was still very early in my sobriety and was adjusting to being with my own thoughts and feelings, but I quickly felt like a trapped animal. I felt buried alive and found it hard to concentrate. I had a few books I wanted to read, but I could barely concentrate on what I was reading without an overwhelming sense of impending doom and panic. In this disturbing state, sleep was surprisingly hard to come by. Of course, it didn't help that it was never dark. When I was finally able to fall asleep, I had constant dreams about the prison flooding. I would jolt awake right before the water filled my cell, and even after I realized it was a dream, I still couldn't shake the fear.

All of this distracted me from everything I tried to think about and reflect on. My life over the previous months was full of chaos, and I desperately wanted to find a way out. But now, alone in solitary confinement, the panic came in unpredictable waves, whether I was asleep or awake. I had never experienced anything like this in my life. The emotions and lack of control made me question everything. Time had never moved more slowly. I was able to regroup for short periods, get lost in a book for a couple of hours or maybe fall asleep for a little while, only to be woken up by a guard yelling at me that it was meal time. As expected, the food was awful.

I fought the anxiety off, and each hour that passed calmly, I considered a success. As the week progressed, I slowly but surely regrouped myself internally. My time in solitary forced me to deal with how my life as a person and a leader had also become very solitary. I was often alone with my thoughts, which caused me to become an anxiety-ridden leader who on the face of it looked good, but behind the scenes was a mess. While I was desperate to get out of solitary and felt as if a weight had been lifted when I was released, I also came to realize that the time in solitary gave me a great deal of time to reflect. It created a deep-seated belief that I can do anything I put my mind to. While there are certainly tougher things to accomplish in life, for me, this was the most challenging experience I had even been through mentally. It gave me the confidence to re-create my life, both personally and professionally. It was the beginning of my personal transformation and of the book you are holding in your hands today.

I've thought about this experience often since then, particularly the mental and emotional side of the challenge, as I've gone through other difficult circumstances in my life and at work. Our challenges and setbacks are like anything else in life—we build up a tolerance to the pain, to the hurt, and to the doubt. I don't believe we overcome those things, at least in the sense that we defeat them. We overcome them by walking with them, by welcoming them, and by understanding that the feeling can be present but not in control. I find the same application in many situations, from work circumstances to my marriage, my family, and my community.

The day I walked out of jail was a new beginning for me. I don't pretend everything changed on that day, and I certainly still don't have all the answers. But I discovered a newfound freedom as I began to recalibrate my life. Since that day, I've learned a lot more about myself as a leader, and I'm eager to introduce you to new ways to lead, no longer alone, but in community with others who want to help each other build healthy organizations.

My goal in writing this book is to share my story in hopes that others can learn from my experience or the lessons I've learned the hard way. By no means do I pretend to have all the answers or that I execute flawlessly all of these concepts. The following pages are a collection of ideas, experiences, and thoughts that I believe are a unique and needed approach to leadership. I hope you enjoy!

CHAPTER 1

Deconstruct Your Silo

*"If you want to go fast, go alone.
If you want to go far, go together."*

—*African proverb*

Nothing is worse for a leader than feeling alone in the midst of many challenges. It's a common problem. As communication breaks down and the separation between you, your organization, and your problems grow, so does your frustration. It's a vicious circle, and the gap eventually becomes a canyon without a bridge.

What if I told you that your feelings of abandonment within the organization you lead are self-inflicted?

What if I told you the best thing you can do for yourself today is to get out of your own way?

The word "silo" refers either to a tower that a farmer uses to store grain or an underground chamber in which a guided missile is kept ready for firing. It's also a common business metaphor for separate divisions or departments that stockpile information and seal it in. Organizational silos often refer to divisions that operate independently and avoid sharing information. It also refers to business departments with silo system applications in which information cannot be shared because of system limitations. Either way, silos contribute to ineffective management and they inhibit growth.

Leaders often lament that their organizations are silo-ridden and look for solutions to increase sharing across all levels. But they often fail to look in the mirror. When a leader builds a silo, so does everyone else who works for the CEO. The greater problem is that the leader's silo mentality trickles down to the rest of the organization. Have you built a silo? You may not even realize it. The CEO silo is probably the most insidious because you build it unbeknownst to yourself, and everyone else on your team is afraid to tell you so. It sneaks up on you and then bites you in the ass. Your silo is largely what's standing in your way toward being an effective leader AND being satisfied at work.

How often do we read or hear about stories of CEOs whose large and successful organizations crumbled in a sudden and even shocking way? From Enron to WorldCom to Lehman Brothers, each organization was headed by a leader whose silo was so impenetrable that he was completely blindsided by the chaos all around him. In each case, the CEO's personal life also suffered a huge toll.

I believe one of the most important steps you can take to better manage your organization and your own sense of well-being and fulfillment as a leader is to deconstruct your own silo. But before you can begin to recognize the walls that surround you, you will have to do something tough. You will have to acknowledge to yourself that you aren't the great leader you might think you are. You might have to admit the challenges you're facing were of your own creation, and the skills that helped you create these challenges won't help you fix it. Let me explain.

I have participated in a peer learning group for nonprofit CEOs in our area for the last few years. Each year we have a few new participants as people change jobs, etc. It is always a good reminder when I talk with people who are new to their CEO seats. I was that person (and in many ways I still am). We worked so hard to get to these jobs. It was thrilling to be offered the job and to get started and then smack!—reality hits you square in the nose, the stinging kind that makes your eyes water and your nose run. That was definitely not what I expected.

As the great fighter Mike Tyson once said, "Everyone has a plan until they get punched in the mouth." (Our plans can go out the window.) Most of us react in one of two ways: essentially fight or flight. We either engage in the tension or we retreat. Finding a balance is tough, particularly if you are new to a leadership role. I'll get into this more throughout the book, but we have more options when it comes to responding.

When I was in solitary confinement, I learned one thing very quickly: Being alone might seem to be a good idea because you're free from everyone else in your life who agitates you, stands in your way, or otherwise causes you stress, but it turns out to be the absolute worst place possible. I also figured out that I was the guy responsible for my own current state of abandonment. I built my own cell. CEOs and other business leaders often build their own cells, their silos. Your problem isn't whether or not you're a genius; it's that you built a silo and you've fooled yourself into thinking that you don't need other people.

Is this you?

- You don't share or seek honest information from your team.
- You dictate and play from the top down, relying on your make-believe prowess.
- You spend most of your day sitting behind your desk, looking at dashboards.
- You don't know much about the personal lives of your team members.
- You get angry when you're the last to discover problems in your organization.
- You're blindsided when key people suddenly resign.
- You don't know who to trust anymore.
- You hold all your meetings in your own office or your conference room.

If you can answer "yes" to any of these questions, then it's time for you to own up to yourself and to deconstruct your silo. Of course, it feels lonely at the top! You've effectively boxed yourself in.

The silo mindset does not appear accidentally, nor is it a coincidence. When you lead an organization, it's only natural to adjust communicating with the people you lead, trying to balance what they need to be aware of with what they need to know to do their work. Managing people is hard work. Dealing with all the personalities and their idiosyncratic behavior can be complex and exhausting. If your organization is larger, staff members often come and go, making it even harder to get a handle on who's doing what. Leading people is not for the faint of heart. But unless and until you welcome people into your sphere of influence, you will live in a silo that will eventually be a very lonely and ineffective place to lead from.

Your silo is a mentality you develop as a self-defense mechanism. You intuitively know that problems that can be solved by sharing them with your team, but you still do not make the connection with them because you're afraid of the self-perceived hard work. So the basic action of reaching out and asking for help does not happen. It may be because it is embarrassing to ask for help, or because it leaves you exposed when leaders fight for the top positions in the leadership team. Or maybe it's because you easily lose patience with people. Whatever the reason, you're essentially protecting your made-up genius by refusing to share information or knowledge with the people in your organization. Your silo seems comfortable at first because it minimizes the uncomfortable conversations and decisions you must make. When you're alone in your silo you literally start to pretend certain people and situations are fine or don't exist, disaster lurks. The greater problem is that your silo mentality trickles down to the rest of your organization. When you build yourself a silo, so does everyone else. Then you're in real trouble!

Jim Hauden, best-selling business author and chairman of Root Inc., believes that business success isn't just the result of great strategy and execution, but it comes by meaningful connection with the people inside your organization: "There is a way to create real collaboration," he writes. "You have to let go. You have to loosen your grip on being right or on winning. You almost need to enter a conversation with no point of view, ready to receive others' ideas and then layer your thoughts on top of them. By approaching a conversation this way, you'll wind up with solutions you never thought of before." That's great advice.

So how do you deconstruct your silo?

Mark Twain once wrote, "It ain't what you *don't* know that gets you into trouble. It's what you know for sure that just ain't so." It is what you know for sure, the things you are certain of that turn out not to be true, that get you into trouble. So the first thing is to acknowledge that you might not know it all. Sure, you built a company or you flew up the corporate ladder to a leadership position, but we all succeed with the help and support of others. No one has accomplished anything alone. So first, acknowledge that all the knowledge doesn't reside just with you.

The second thing is to solicit feedback. Unsolicited, surprise feedback is often received as criticism, even if there is only a small hint of negativity in it. If you tell the waiter that his service was not so good, but he did not ask, he is likely to feel criticized. If he asks for feedback, he is likely to take the same comments positively. Solicited feedback is much more often appreciated. Ask others for candid feedback on a regular basis. Don't surprise people (particularly people who work for you) by asking them for feedback when they don't expect to provide it. Make soliciting feedback an expected part of your relationship with your coworkers, and then receive it in a constructive way.

Third, don't beat people up with your power. People know who is in charge, so don't beat them up with reminders. I once sat in a room with a leader and his team while he reminded them over and over that he was in charge. He decided who got plum assignments and who did not, and they had nothing to say about it. He won, but he defeated his team that day, and for the rest of his tenure.

Leaders are often more subtle than this in reminding everyone who is in charge, but still the message of "I am in charge and you are not" is very clear. Check your behavior to see if you are sending such messages unintentionally.

How does this translate to day-to-day activity? I've tried to work on a few things in my regular schedule that can help reinforce these behaviors. I have developed a few ideas to adjust your daily approach to your role. While the first reaction to most problems often will be to store it inside your silo, fight that urge. Here's what I suggest you do on a daily basis:

- **Remember your primary role,** which is to coach, develop, motivate, and inspire your staff. People are relying on you to fill that role. When problems build up, the tension is often high, and I feel as if it's all on my shoulders. I will go into someone else's office and find a way to help. It is a confidence booster trick for me, but I've found that it helps me return to work with my shoulders a little lighter.
- **Leave the hubris at the door.** You don't know it all, and you can't do it all. Your job is not to

outdo everyone else. You already "made it," so don't feel that you have to continually impress. Instead of trying to fix things yourself, let go a little bit. You might be surprised that your team knows more than you do about fixing problems. It's also unfair to expect everyone to work for Captain America. It's too much pressure, and it contributes to people not wanting to work with you.

- **Manage your insecurities.** Everyone has insecurities, especially leaders, but great leaders don't inflict them on their people. If you are looking at your staff as an extension of your insecurities, then all you will do is demotivate those around you. When a CEO literally feels threatened by his own staff, it is a sure sign of a looming problem. Micromanagers are insecure and don't survive for long. If you feel insecurity creep up on you, the best way to stuff it back down is to share it with someone else. Try opening up with your staff about your own lack of knowledge in an area, and you might be surprised at how honest your team suddenly becomes with you.

- **Loosen your grip.** Riding a horse well requires holding the reins loosely; swinging a golf club well requires holding the club loosely. You can feel what is going on with the horse or the golf club much better when you hold the reins or the club loosely. You already bemoan the fact that you don't control as much as you'd like, so why not just give up a little more? CEOs who are wound tightly with tempers flaring are no good to anyone.

- **Focus on the big picture.** The problem with a silo is that you obsess about details and get hung up on issues that drag you into negative thinking. Yes, there are more problems within your organization than you know how to deal with. But if you spend most of your day chasing fires, the place will appear to be burning down. So rather than focusing on the darkness of the micro, spend more of your day focused on the light of the big future. Constantly tell the story of how great your organization is, both internally and externally.

- **Walk around.** Get out of your office—frequently.

CHAPTER 2

Everything Will Be OK

"Things work out best for those that make the best of the way that things work out."

—John Wooden

Our organization was in a really tough spot. Revenue was trending down. Funding that was out of our control was in serious jeopardy. Expenses weren't sustainable, and the competition was on our tail. Management was attuned to the problems at hand, but we had not revealed them to the entire staff yet. We needed people to be aware of our situation. Our goal was to create urgency, but the ensuing staff meeting was a lesson I'll never forget about sharing news, particularly bad news, with the team.

In an effort to motivate the team to grind through our current challenges and step up effort, management decided to offer up a doomsday scenario. The tone of the message went something like this: Things were bad, really bad, and if the team didn't work harder, things would soon get even worse. We sensed tension and unease begin to grow in the room. While our message was not completely inaccurate (the organization was facing serious jeopardy), the tone and delivery were excessively negative and sounded hopeless.

As I glanced around the room during the all-staff meeting, I could see the fear in people's eyes. I could sense them tightening. When we suggested to our team that the organization might crumble, they naturally began to think more about their own personal livelihoods than the life of the organization. That wasn't a bridge too far, and I could tell that management erred by taking the "sky-is-falling" path. During the presentation, I wasn't so sure that management understood the impact it was having on the team. I could sense the message was being received as a sudden knee-jerk reaction to problems we knew could be solved.

When it was my time to speak, I decided to throw out the script. Pieces of the upcoming challenges were my responsibility, so I had to be transparent, but I also had to read the room. Without permission, I gave the team a contrarian message. I was not the CEO at this particular moment, so it was admittedly a bit uncomfortable to go against the grain. But I stood up and confidently told the staff this simple message: "Everything will be OK." Instead of the apocalyptic message everyone else was sharing, I assured the team that although we were facing some challenges, we would survive and even thrive. It was not the end of our organization and surely not the end of the world. Together we'd move ahead and figure out these problems. "These are serious issues, and the organization needs to be focused on them," I said. "But that isn't what each of you needs to be stressed about. All of us need to be focused on doing the best we can in our own roles; we can't all solve these problems. If we each play our role, I assure you, everything will be OK."

As my colleagues in upper management squirmed in their chairs, I could feel the tension come out of the room a little bit. I knew I made the right decision when I saw smiles, uncrossed arms, and nodding heads. Afterwards, when challenged about my rosy presentation, I held my own and punted the ball back: "Our job as leaders is to carry that burden, not to share it with everyone else. People need clarity. They need to understand what we are facing, but they also need confidence that their leaders are in control." Again, I was not the CEO at the time, but it was a moment I won't forget, and it's a lesson I learned and still use today.

When things get tough, are you the company's Chief Naysayer Officer? Or are you the one who finds a way to deliver bad news in a way that inspires and motivates your team?

We all know naysayers, gloomy people who spend too much time in the dark. Leaders can sometimes be the worst at this. All too often, leaders choose to present their staff with less than optimistic pictures in the face of challenges. Whether it's a missed sales forecast, disappointing earnings, problems in HR, the sudden rise of a new competitor, or the resignation of a key employee, it's important to deliver bad news with honesty but also with as much optimism as you can muster, given the situation. And most of the time, the situation is *not dire*.

Why do CEOs and senior management sometimes tend to go negative when delivering tough news?

In our desperation to create urgency in our teams, we often choose the route of scare tactics. We assume people will respond to a threat to their livelihood by digging deeper, when the reality is that people will save themselves by leaving you to sink alone on the ship.

I also believe the reasons are rooted in the leaders' own lack of confidence, both in themselves and in their own people, and also in their lack of fulfillment and enjoyment in their own roles. They project their own insecurities, dissatisfaction, and fears on others.

Webster defines a naysayer as "A person who distrusts other people and believes that everything is done for selfish reasons." A naysayer is not simply someone with a bad attitude, but someone who inherently believes he has all the answers. Does that sound like a CEO you know? Maybe that's you in the mirror!

When I talk to colleagues, I ask questions to survey their self-awareness. Are you becoming a self-fulfilling prophecy? Is the company *truly* in dire straits, or is the CEO in dire straits? They say that preachers are often preaching to themselves. I think the same is true for CEOs and other leaders who focus too much on what's going wrong rather than on what's going right with their organizations.

I've discovered three effective ways a leader can deliver messages that have a positive impact on their teams. These are a few simple yet important things to keep in mind when delivering news about challenges in the company.

First and foremost, it's almost never helpful to go negative with your team. Yes, sometimes there are situations that call for it. But by and large, it truly is a fact that "Everything is going to be OK." Act like it, and be like it. Your team needs to feel it. The more confidence they have that there WILL be a future, the more they will act like it. On the other hand, the less confident they are, chances are they will think more about their next job than about how to protect their current job.

Don't get me wrong here—I'm not saying you present everything as rainbows and butterflies or that your teams are above criticism. That definitely isn't the case. But HOW you present the negative is what matters. Leadership needs to be clear-eyed about the problems, but they must be prepared to share it only when there are also action-oriented solutions and ways for people to contribute.

Stephen Sample, author of the *New York Times* bestseller *The Contrarian's Guide to Leadership*, writes,

"Congenital naysayers are among the greatest stumbling blocks to thinking free. Rather than imagining how a new idea might possibly work, they instinctively think of all the reasons why it won't. They sincerely believe that they are doing everyone a favor by reducing the amount of time spent on bad or foolish ideas. But what they really do is undermine the creativity that can be harvested from thinking free." I believe this is exactly what management was doing when conveying their doomsday scenario above. Rather than skipping the "sky-is-falling" part and moving on to creative solutions, they camped out on the negative because they didn't trust the team to create solutions in the first place. Trust your team, and they will trust you.

Always remember that people tend to point fingers in a corporate landscape. Part of your role as a leader is to create a culture that doesn't pass blame but fixes problems. You can do this by passing over bad news and embracing good news. If you're always reminding your team of what's working, they'll be less likely to shift blame and instead be champions of your organization.

Second, admit to yourself that this will be hard work and that it will always be hard work. If you're new to the CEO role, you need to accept that it doesn't only start out hard but that it will get even harder. That is not doomsday; it's simply a reality. The longer you lead an organization, the harder it gets, particularly if it's a growing organization. I believe that "lonely at the top" feelings are fed by a false notion that the CEO's job should be more glamorous. The CEO's role gets romanticized, and then when it feels more like being in the trenches than you thought it would be, the disillusionment sets in. The first step toward defeating the disillusionment is to stop being illusioned!

Tell yourself every day: I've got a tough job. There will be bad news. Acknowledge to yourself that you indeed do have the toughest job in your organization. You're paid more than your staff because you agreed to shoulder and share in everyone else's burdens. The CEO's job is to solve problems, big problems. But it's also true that you often don't have a better idea than anyone else on your team.

Admit these things to yourself:

- There will be more scars than trophies.
- Your mistakes will be glaring.
- You have to wear many hats all at once.
- The team will not be completely honest with you.
- Key people will quit on a moment's notice.
- People will criticize you behind your back.

Rather than look for a way out of your hard job, which is essentially why you go negative in the first place, start to accept it and relish in it. Yes, your job is hard, but you love it! Remember, you've always loved a challenge, and you didn't get to where you are by going after easy things. Stop playing games with yourself, pretending that it's harder than you expected. When you go into the office every day looking to solve hard problems, knowing full well that it won't be easy, then you'll start to look at your doomsday scenarios in a different light. You'll view them as challenges that must be and will be conquered, rather than obstacles that are driving you to hate your work.

Finally, remind yourself that few decisions you make are life-altering or even organization-altering. The sky is not falling, and you rarely need to act as if it is. You don't have to make all the decisions today. You have to make only one decision. Also, you don't have to make every decision today.

CHAPTER 3

Go Back to the Basics

*"The last of human freedoms—the ability
to choose one's attitude in a given
set of circumstances."*

—Viktor E. Frankl

One of the biggest challenges I've faced personally as I've grown into leadership roles, or even simply as our organization has grown over the last few years, has been to maintain control over my schedule and workload. I'm not talking so much about task lists or project priorities as much as the demands on my time and attention. Filtering what deserves my specific attention versus what doesn't, and what should be either ignored or handed off to someone else, is a much underestimated challenge in a leadership role.

In my experience, this type of pressure on my availability—both in terms of time and attention—can change as I take on more work, but it also varies month to month as the organization goes through changes. It can become overwhelming. The only way I have found to overcome it is to go back to the basics of what got me here, and to reset a little bit.

I spend a lot of time with my daughters in the backyard shooting baskets. (Going through their drills and practice they can get frustrating if one of them misses a few shots in a row.) As you might imagine, the frustration doesn't help her to make the next shot. It clouds her thinking and is a distraction. She gets a little more tense and her form falls apart, which leads to more missed shots. There is nothing productive about it. The solution? Pause, take a breath, and move closer to the basket. She focuses on her form and a few shots will go in. There's something about seeing the ball go through the basket, even from five feet away, that helps build her confidence right back to where it belongs.

The same principle is true in the rest of our lives.

I have this experience fairly regularly at work with my own workload and stress, and I see it in others. The demands (either real or self-inflicted) get to be a little too much, and I have no more control. What does this look like at work? The calendar will be over-scheduled, email will be unread, and there will be no time to think or plan.

When this happens, the "basketball practice" principle has been my saving grace. I step back from the whirlwind a little bit and get back to basics. For example, when the whirlwind gets a little intense for me, I spend time on some of the things related to the role that may have been handed off or I haven't gotten a chance to do in a while. My first job ever was washing dishes at a pizza restaurant in a small town in Iowa. Years later, I was working in management for a food service company, and when the management tasks and work became a bit much, I would sneak back to the dish room and tell the workers to take a break. I would then get to work doing that job for 20 to 30 minutes.

You might be surprised what working on that type of thing can do for your stress level!

Before I became sober, I had motivation and some discipline about many things in life, but alcohol wasn't one of them. My solution to a lot of things, from anxiety to things not going well at work, was to drink. This obviously wasn't a sustainable stress management tactic, and I paid the price in a major way.

Some of the foundational principles of recovery and maintaining sobriety can also be helpful in how we manage other areas of life and stress.

SET SMALL AND ACHIEVABLE GOALS

In recovery, they talk about days. Days are important. I struggled with this more than with not drinking. For the first six months, it served as a reminder of all the harm I caused and all the bad decisions I made. I had many conversations with friends and family about this exact thing. They would say things like, "Congratulations! One hundred days sober," which never felt great to me. All I heard was "Congratulations! It's been one hundred days since you royally messed something up." I know that wasn't anyone's intent, but it was how I saw myself and how I defined the days.

The point, though, in being worried about the days is that they string into weeks, months, and years. Now at ten years of sobriety, I don't count the days, but the days still matter.

Aristotle said, "We are what we repeatedly do," and the same is true with how we manage our workload, the way we interact with people, and how we approach leadership.

ELIMINATE TEMPTATION

As I was beginning to work through sobriety, I wanted to maintain as much of a normal life as possible. After all, I was recently divorced and was trying to figure out how to date in this new world of not drinking, so I tried to continue life as close to normal as possible. At first, I thought the anxiety and pressure around being in a bar or other triggering place would pass if I just pushed through. It turned out not to be the case for me. I distinctly remember a trip to New Orleans with a chamber of commerce program I was in. I had decided (like many of the participants) to tack on another day to the trip to explore and hang out in New Orleans. We were staying on Bourbon Street, and most evenings, we ended up at one of the bars near our hotel.

My anxiety on the trip was paralyzing. On the extra day that I stayed, I don't think I left my hotel room. Yes, I know there is plenty to see in New Orleans that doesn't require drinking or going to a bar, but the anxiety and pressure were more than I could handle. I spent an entire extra day and night in New Orleans reading and watching TV in my hotel room, essentially acting as if I weren't there. I didn't respond to text messages from my colleagues in the group; I essentially just froze.

What I learned the hard way, though, was that some things I could not just power through. I had to actively set up the structure to eliminate the temptation. If I don't have my favorite cookies in the house, I won't eat them for dessert every night.

BUILD ROUTINE

A consistent and steady routine really is an avenue to self-care. We function better in routine, and while your days as a leader can sometimes be all over the place, routine can be your saving grace. At the core of this, particularly when I was new to recovery, the three biggest routines are sleep, exercise, and nutrition.

As Rachel Goldman, Ph.D., a psychologist and clinical assistant professor at the NYU School of Medicine, explains: "If people don't have structure and are sitting around with less to focus on, then they also probably will find themselves thinking about the stressful situation more, which can also lead to additional stress and anxiety. A lack of structure and routine can actually exacerbate feelings of distress and make you pay more attention to the source of your problems." That's what I mean about a vicious circle. Just because you're a leader, it doesn't excuse you from having to deal with all the little stuff in your life. It will still be there the day after your promotion, and unless you find a better way to deal with it, it will kill you.

But if you can find a consistent way to think about the big things, you'd not only be happier and healthier, but you'd also be a lot smarter, right? You'd be more approachable, which would free up your creative space. You'd finally have time to think about the things you want to think about and to do the things you want to do. Your spouse and children would love you for it, too, because you'll be more present. You don't yell at your kids because of the big things, do you? It's all the little things that make you angry. What would it be like to have more control over your own thoughts and actions?

The way to find a consistent way to better deal with the big things in your life is to become more regimented. I believe the key is to create a routine that adds structure and a sense of predictability to your day. Of course, your schedule may change somewhat depending on the day of the week, but sticking to a basic structure for when you will wake, eat, work, do activities, and sleep can help you feel less stressed and more organized. Structuring your day also ensures that you accomplish the basic tasks that must be done, which will leave you with the time to schedule in other things that you want or need to accomplish.

Take pride in your ability to say "no" to those things that interrupt your boxes. For example, I start my day with a workout routine, and I don't let anything or anyone get in my way. It's top priority. It makes me feel better and more focused, so it's a part of my regimen.

Timothy Ferriss suggested in his book, *The 4-Hour Workweek*, "The timing is never right. For all of the most important things, the timing always sucks." I fight this battle every day. It always feels as if there's just not quite enough time in the workday. It can become a real point of frustration that can lead me to throw up my hands and retreat. But I've found that if I can create more order and regimen into my life, I find the time I've been looking for.

According to the Pareto Principle, recommended by Tim Ferriss himself, roughly 80 percent of your outcomes (or your outputs) result from only 20 percent of all your causes (or your inputs) for any given event.

This means if you're spending more than 20 percent of your time on the little things, it's making you an unproductive person. You're unable to reach your outcomes because you're obsessed with unnecessary inputs. In business, a goal of this 80/20 rule is to identify inputs that are potentially the most productive and make them the priority. For instance, once you identify the key factors that are most critical to your company's success, you should give those factors the most focus, not all the other inconsequential things you spin your wheels doing every day. At its core, the 80/20 rule is about identifying an entity's best assets and using them efficiently to create maximum value. This is, of course, not a revolutionary concept. In fact, it's rather obvious. But if you're drowning simply because you lost your keys again, you'll always be looking for a lifeline.

CHAPTER 4

Become the Third Person in Your Life

"Don't become too preoccupied with what is happening around you. Pay more attention to what is going on within you."

—Mary-Frances Winters

If

by Rudyard Kipling

If you can keep your head when all about you
   Are losing theirs and blaming it on you,
If you can trust yourself when all men doubt you,
   But make allowance for their doubting too;
If you can wait and not be tired by waiting,
   Or being lied about, don't deal in lies,
Or being hated, don't give way to hating,
   And yet don't look too good, nor talk too wise:

If you can dream—and not make dreams
          your master;
If you can think—and not make thoughts your aim;
If you can meet with Triumph and Disaster
   And treat those two impostors just the same;
If you can bear to hear the truth you've spoken
   Twisted by knaves to make a trap for fools,
Or watch the things you gave your life to, broken,
   And stoop and build 'em up with worn-out tools:

If you can make one heap of all your winnings
   And risk it on one turn of pitch-and-toss,
And lose, and start again at your beginnings

And never breathe a word about your loss;
If you can force your heart and nerve and sinew
To serve your turn long after they are gone,
And so hold on when there is nothing in you
Except the Will which says to them: "Hold on!"

If you can talk with crowds and keep your virtue,
Or walk with Kings—nor lose the common touch,
If neither foes nor loving friends can hurt you,
If all men count with you, but none too much;
If you can fill the unforgiving minute
With sixty seconds' worth of distance run,
Yours is the Earth and everything that's in it,
And—which is more—you'll be a Man, my son!

I first heard this poem by Rudyard Kipling when I was eleven or twelve years old. I was captivated by it then. While I'm spilling a lot of ink here with my take on leadership, Kipling does it succinctly in thirty-two lines.

If you can meet with Triumph and Disaster; and treat those two *imposters* just the same…

I find myself regularly referring to this poem when I'm faced with challenges at work, or even in my personal life. The profound sentiment is the call for balance and how that balance can be incredibly hard to maintain as we move through our careers. Success can be had, but remain true to yourself even while walking with kings and not losing your common touch.

———— ∞ ————

There was no easier place than a jail cell for me to sulk, to feel sorry for myself, to blame others, and to continue down the same selfish path that got me there. I spent my time in a muddy state of self-pity, running circles in my brain, and convincing myself that no one in the world had it worse. This was especially easy to do when I was sitting there all by myself, day after day, surrounded by other people all doing the same thing. My thoughts soon become exaggeratedly negative and turned into a vicious circle of self-paralyzing inactivity.

I use jail as a metaphor for leaders as a way to think about becoming a better leader and a happier person. But it was also a real experience. It really happened to me. You might be an aspiring leader and might look at me today and say, "I want to do what he does." But as John Maxwell once said, "If you're going to do what I do, then you have to do what I did!"

So what did I do? How did I escape my own hell?

Jail was where I discovered freedom and a better way to think and feel about myself. It's where I learned how to separate myself from my cell. Separating from myself was, in fact, the only way out. I had to own it.

It's time for you to start owning it, too, to become the third person in your life.

Believe it or not, many business leaders I know struggle with similar feelings of being trapped. They feel jailed emotionally, mentally, spiritually, or even physically. Being at the top of an organization can make you feel as if you're in your own special little prison. You might not be locked away in a five-by-eight cell with no windows, but emotionally you feel completely trapped in a situation with no way out. You lock yourself in your office, you don't talk about it at home, and your thoughts go into a loop.

Be honest with yourself. Does this sometimes sound like you?

You've reached the "top," but you harbor feelings of self-pity. In fact, as you climbed your corporate ladder, these feelings have actually intensified, which probably has come as a surprise to you. Your goal was to be a manager, a supervisor, a director, a vice president, a president and CEO, or maybe even an owner. The allure of more money, more respect, and more control meant that you'd feel much better about yourself. But rather than basking in the glory, the weight of responsibility began to outweigh the glitter and gold. Rather than confront each day with confidence, you find ways to just get through it, hoping nobody will notice.

Maybe this is still a subconscious feeling, and you're just now beginning to realize it. It took me a while to realize it, too. It took a jail cell for me to fully comprehend it and then to find a better way.

When I sat in my jail cell, I realized that wallowing in self-pity was an exhausting way to live. And I'd been there for too long. Weirdly (or not so weirdly) enough, making myself the center of the universe is a lot of work. It requires twisting reality to fit a narrative that is detrimental, and quite frankly, not true. When I looked around at my jail mates, I realized that I was not one of them. I knew that I was better than this, and that my enemy was not actually anything or anyone else. I admitted to myself that I had become the enemy, and it was time to remove myself from myself, to begin to look at myself as an observer, and to become the third person in my life. This is when and where I began to disconnect from myself.

Have you ever wondered why you're able to give better advice to others than to yourself? That's because you see yourself as the center of the universe. You're "Captain Me Planet," and you rarely disconnect from yourself. It can be a good thing when you're trying to help someone else with his problems, but it's a bad thing when you're trying to help yourself.

To begin to feel better about yourself and your role as a leader, you have to get to the point in life where

I was in my jail cell, where you stop feeling as if the world is out to get you. Your staff, shareholders, board of directors, customers, and vendors are not all out to get you. You are just another person, another CEO, living and working among other people—people whose collective existence can result in situations beyond your control. So get over it. Every day is a new day, and you're defined by the collective impact of your life, *not by a single event*. The CEO is an office, not you!

I have participated for the last few years in a CEO roundtable group, essentially a confidential and private group of nonprofit CEOs who get together monthly for learning opportunities, sharing, and engagement. One exercise we do each month is case studies. We take turns sharing challenges we are facing at work that we think our colleagues could help us with. Maybe not so surprisingly, other people's problems are always much easier to solve than our own. Without exception, I would leave those meetings with a different perspective on how to solve the issues I was facing at the office after hearing the valuable feedback and input from others.

Abraham Lincoln once wrote, "I claim not to have controlled events, but confess plainly that events have controlled me." What a great place to be, right? Perhaps it is simpler to blame an outside force for the things that unravel in your life. It's certainly far more interesting to cast blame, isn't it? You can spend countless hours assigning each individual thing and person who put you in your cell. Or you can turn inward and begin to accept the blame. In one fell swoop, boom, you found the problem: You!

Though you are not completely in control of what happens to you, you can recognize that you have the power to dictate your response. You don't have to be subject to a false narrative about your life or an unseeable future. Rather, you can rest in the fact that only you are in charge of yourself. Own it. If you're as mentally tough as you think you are, then begin to recognize when you're at risk of becoming caught in a downward spiral of self-pity. Be the third person when it comes to your problems. Stop being the victim, and give yourself the same kind of advice you'd give to a friend.

Most of the advice you dole out, you're forgetting to say to yourself. As a CEO or business leader, your job is to take control, not just of everything around you, but also of yourself. Be your own friend, and begin to give yourself your best advice.

CHAPTER 5

Players Take the Wins, Coaches Take the Losses

"Opportunity often comes disguised in the form of misfortune, or temporary defeat."

—*Napoleon Hill*

When thinking about or discussing business challenges with coworkers and colleagues, I find myself using sports analogies, particularly team sports. I grew up playing sports, sticking with basketball through college. I find that the older I get, the more the analogies seem to make sense. I recognize these aren't always the most inclusive analogies, but I think people who grew up playing team sports can relate to many of the dynamics.

While a lot goes on behind the scenes within a sports team, there is also a significant amount that plays out in the public. After each game, the coach and many players have to sit and answer questions from the media. You see very quickly how people manage success and failure.

I also believe viewing or playing sports offers us an opportunity to see how some problems are best solved, not on the court or field, but in the office. Many of the same lessons we learn from sports can also be applied to the business world, but in simpler ways that are easier to break down and think about. There are a number of (complex) ways to keep score in business, but there's only one way to keep the score in a football or basketball game. Unless the game is a tie, there's always a winner, and after a game is over, analysts can usually pinpoint why a particular team won or lost. In fact, we spend a great deal of time, post-game, talking about it. But in the business world, the winners and losers aren't always so clear.

Let me offer you an example of what we can learn from the world of sports in terms of leadership. This example pains me every time I think about it, but there's much to learn from it.

I'm from Kansas City, so I have been thoroughly enjoying the Chiefs' run the last few years. The Chiefs had lost only two games during the regular season and entered Super Bowl LV favored to win. The party had already started in Kansas City before the game even began on Sunday, February 21, 2021. Then, ouch. The Chiefs were completely undone by offensive struggles and costly penalties. For the first time all season, our pro-bowl quarterback, Patrick Mahomes, failed to score a single touchdown, and the team lost to Tom Brady and the Buccaneers by double digits, making the Chiefs only the third Super Bowl team to not score a touchdown. The final score was 31–9. It was definitely ugly.

Here's where the business lesson comes into play. After the game, head coach Andy Reid, the fifth winningest coach in NFL history, was asked what happened. How did the winningest team all season long lose so badly? "They played better than we did,"

Reid said. "That's my responsibility, and I take full responsibility for it. You just can't do the things that we did and beat a good football team like that, particularly at this level." Reid walked the plank. He threw himself under the bus. He was the self-expressed fall guy.

Anyone who watched Super Bowl LV could plainly see that this wasn't a coaching problem. Was the Buccaneers' defensive game plan better than the Chiefs' offense? Maybe. But what was most clear was that the Chiefs' offensive line was outmatched. They didn't have the talent or ability to effectively protect their own quarterback. Mahomes spent more time being chased by the Buccaneers' defense than he did finding a wide-open receiver. Not a coach in the history of the NFL could have prevented what happened. Eleven stronger and faster guys on the defense beat eleven weaker and slower guys on the offense.

But Andy Reid owned it. He took responsibility. He was in charge, and he took the heat for a big loss in a big moment. He placed the burden on his own shoulders. This is what I mean when I say that sports can often offer us a clear example of a business challenge. Reid gave us, in one fell swoop, an example of what leadership means. Reid did what most leaders are not prepared to do: take the blame, even publicly.

We see the opposite happen all the time in the private sector, in government, and in the public square. It's all too common.

Volkswagen's CEO Michael Horn blamed a "rogue employee" to explain how the cars' engine software cheated in pollution tests. Horn was later fired for lying and covering it up. Boeing's former chairman, David Calhoun, became CEO after the board fired Dennis Muilenburg. Then less than two months later, Calhoun blamed everyone, including Muilenburg, for the company's 737 MAX crisis. Calhoun kept his job, but he was summarily criticized for his words. In the public square, we can look to the example of President Donald J. Trump. For a person who was known for saying, "I only hire the best people," history documents that Trump fired fifty-five people for problems and mistakes that took place under his tenure. This was not a surprise since he took on celebrity status for firing people on his popular television show, *The Apprentice*. The list goes on and on. In the face of failure, many leaders often try to shift the blame.

This is not responsible leadership. A true leader doesn't pass the blame for failure but graciously accepts responsibility for the problems he inherited or that occurred on his watch. Leading with integrity means taking personal responsibility. It's tempting for people to take flight and avoid the personal consequences of what happened, to reject personal responsibility, and to pass the blame on to other people. In the case of Boeing's Calhoun, he could have acknowledged that the board's actions had a role in the situation. By facing up to these criticisms and admitting that Boeing and its board could have done things better, Calhoun could have encouraged others at Boeing to do the same, especially considering that he must overhaul the company culture from the top down.

Jim Collins' book, *Good to Great*, is one of the most iconic business and leadership books of all time. You've probably read it. I think one of Collins' most adept observations is how he explores the leadership traits that exist in CEOs that take companies from good to great. He writes about the levels of leadership: a highly capable individual, a contributing team member, a competent manager, an effective leader, and a Level 5 executive. Many leaders aspire, yet fail, to be a Level 5 executive because they forget the difference between the Levels 4 and 5.

The difference is how "effective leaders" (Level 4) and Level 5 leaders channel their talents and ambitions. Level 4 leaders often function in an egotistical, self-serving manner. Meanwhile, Level 5 leaders operate in a spirit of service to others and to the mission, channeling their ego away from themselves and focusing on building a great company. Level 5 leaders are ambitious and driven but focused on building a great company and not their own personal brand or wealth. They balance their drive and determination with a humble approach.

According to Collins, there is a difference in levels of success between professional will and personal humility. Personal humility includes acting with calm, quiet determination; shunning opportunities for public recognition, praise, or accolades; and in tough times, taking personal responsibility when things turn out poorly. On the other hand, professional will is being fanatically driven to produce excellent results for the company, building the organization up for success in the next generation, and doing what must be done to produce the best long-term results.

At the end of the day, the balance between these two approaches comes down to why the work is being done. Are we pushing for success to satisfy our own ego and put ourselves forward? Or do we strive for success based on a greater mission that we sacrifice ourselves and our egos for?

Before Super Bowl LV, Reid was asked what he planned to do if he won the game. "Yes, I'm going to eat a double cheeseburger if that happens," he said. Who knows where he ended up for dinner, but he definitely used the loss as an opportunity to show real leadership. It worked, too.

The Chiefs' Pro Bowl tight end Travis Kelce was also asked about the loss. Appearing on the NFL Network, Kelce said Super Bowl LV was so "embarrassing" that he and the rest of his team were even more fired up to get back to the big game. "That was pretty embarrassing, man, taking that last loss down there in Tampa, man," he said. "If you're not motivated after taking a shellacking like that, I don't know what's wrong with you. Now I want to win one more Super Bowl than I ever wanted to get one in the first place, and that's everybody in that building, man." Did you get that? Everybody in the building. Reid's personal humility trickled down through the entire organization and turned it into renewed motivation to take responsibility for the loss and for the next year's win.

If you're going to succeed as a leader, there's no way to the top without accepting the blame for the mistakes and missteps made along the way.

CHAPTER 6

Man in the Arena

*"Great things in business are never
done by one person; they're done by
a team of people."*

—*Steve Jobs*

Theodore Roosevelt gave a speech in the Sorbonne, Paris, on April 23, 1910, which has been cited and recited throughout history. Today it's known as the "Man in the Arena" speech, and you've likely read it many times, or at least this part of it. The speech was a wild success and was quickly turned into a book that sold millions of copies across Europe. Here's the part of the speech we all recognize more than one-hundred years later:

> *It is not the critic who counts; not the man who points out how the strong man stumbles, or where the doer of deeds could have done them better. The credit belongs to the man who is actually in the arena, whose face is marred by dust and sweat and blood; who strives valiantly; who errs, who comes short again and again, because there is no effort without error and shortcoming; but who does actually strive to do the deeds; who knows great enthusiasms, the great devotions; who spends himself in a worthy cause; who at the best knows in the end the triumph of high achievement, and who at the worst, if he fails, at least fails while daring greatly, so that his place shall never be*

with those cold and timid souls who neither know victory nor defeat.

Roosevelt presents a compelling picture of a strong leader up against the world, such as a boxer or gladiator who fights even to death while the crowds clamor and jeer for more. He portrays leaders as sole survivors, absorbing all the punches and taking all the risks.

The leader is alone in the fight, as all *real* leaders ought to be.

Is this you? Are you alone against the world? You're fighting them all: your competitors, your vendors, your customers, the government, and even your own staff. Does this sound familiar?

This is where I think a huge flaw is in most interpretations of the speech and what most people take away. Roosevelt never uses the word "alone." He describes one man, but he doesn't say that the man is alone in the arena. Over time, we have morphed the meaning of this to mean that I have to do it alone. Doing it alone is a show of strength. No one should criticize me because no one else is in my seat, and no one is in the same arena that I am. They don't have the same stresses, burdens, or responsibilities.

I once looked at leadership the same way. I was the person at the top of the food chain, the one taking all the risks and carrying the weight of the world on my shoulders. I alone was responsible for my professional and personal successes and failures. How dare you judge me. How dare you suggest to me that you can help. I'm in the arena!

I dug a little deeper into his speech and found that many great leaders, including United States presidents, pointed to the "Man in the Arena" speech, including Richard Nixon. During his resignation speech. Nixon used Roosevelt's words to portray himself as the lonely and dejected leader at the top. This certainly made me wonder if it's such a good idea to climb the ladder by myself and sit atop it alone. That strategy certainly failed Nixon. Maybe Roosevelt didn't intend for his speech to be used by business leaders but as a historical reflection of what was soon to happen in Europe. Even so, I learned the hard way what it means to lead alone.

For me, being the man *alone* in the arena resulted in my being alone in a jail cell. As I stared at myself in the mirror, I realized for the first time in my life that pitting myself against the world was a dead-end street with me losing and the world winning.

At the darkest point in my life, I operated from a mindset that everyone was either out to get me or happy to see me fail. My actions protected me from the shame and secrets that I was carrying out in private. I wouldn't let people get too close to me, and I assumed their worst intent or outcome in any given scenario.

I looked at myself as the fearless leader who should always get his way, because it was me and me alone. Being at the top was a great sacrifice, I thought, and I deserved to be praised for it—and left alone. But the problem was that I was lonely and miserable inside.

Once I left jail, rebooted my life, and eventually took on greater leadership roles in business and in my community, I discovered how detrimental this mindset was to my entire life. I carried too much on my shoulders alone because I thought that was a part of my job. But the pressure became too much, and the internal expectations weren't attainable. I couldn't see beyond my own bubble. To make matters worse, I pushed people away. I thought leaders were supposed to push people out of the way.

Warren G. Bennis, a noted authority on leadership and best-selling author, once suggested, "The myth about leadership is that it's a solitary act, 'it's lonely at the top.' But effective leaders need not to be let alone. We need to be bothered once in a while. How long has it been since you were really bothered? About something important, about something real?"

That's a good question. Do you bother to be bothered? Or do you box yourself in and insist on taking all the bullets, never even asking for help or advice?

Bennis says, "To get people to bother you, you have to bother them. Otherwise, people won't take you seriously. Putting out a suggestion box, advertising an open-door policy, even walking the floors and asking, 'What can we do to improve?'—they're all well intentioned, but, unless there's a deep culture of trust and openness, people won't tell you what they really think."

I believe it often takes more courage to lead with others than to lead alone. The job of a leader is to bring people into the arena with you. They may not share the same spot in the area, but they can and will share their own sweat and blood alongside you.

Finding ways to increase honest dialogue between you and your team, to collaborate with openness, and to delegate with confidence are harder than being the gladiator. But at the end of the day, you'll be a happier person with a healthier team and organization.

CHAPTER 7

Throw Away Your Organizational Chart

"Imagination has a great deal to do with winning."

—*Mike Krzyzewski*

There's nothing more annoying to a CEO than when someone complains about status or role in the organizational chart. What's supposed to provide clarity often breeds dysfunction and even chaos. I understand this can be important for people not in the CEO role, but it can literally bring out the worst in staff and cause frustration in leaders.

A traditional organizational chart shows hierarchical lines of reporting, which imply lines of communication running up and down (and across) the organization. They've existed for more than a century and are a familiar part of any CEO's job. We white board them out, and we even look for software to help us better construct and illustrate neat and clean boxes, circles, and lines. Leaders are anxious to fill holes in their organizational charts, but then they throw their hands in the air when they face the eventual futility of their work.

I challenge you to throw your organizational chart away. For many of you reading this book, you've already filed it away anyway, right? You occasionally retrieve and revisit it, and you wonder why it's not helping you solve your problems. It's time to think about permanently filing it away.

This sounds like the decision could lead to mayhem across your organization, and I'm not suggesting that, but the problem with taking the organizational chart at face value is that you end up trying to architect and manage your team as if members were software, neatly tying their communication within predetermined lines. Then you stop communicating and being real with everyone because you "did your job."

I'm not saying that you should enable a free-for-all across your organization. Conceptually, organizational charts help us make better business decisions by laying out who is in charge and who decides how team members make their decisions, how to allocate tasks, and ultimately who's in charge of what. So there's certainly some need to clarify who's who and what's what. But if you rely on your organizational chart to be your primary source, it's going to backfire on you.

Here's what I started to do, based loosely on the thoughts and actions of legendary NCAA basketball coach John Wooden. Wooden won a whopping ten national championships over a twelve-year period, and during his amazing run, he developed something he called the "Pyramid of Success." It not only fostered amazing loyalty and admiration from former players such as Bill Walton and Lew Alcindor (Kareem Abdul-Jabbar), but it also made him one of the most revered coaches in the history of sports.

Here's what Wooden believed. He discovered that people perform best when they achieved a "peace of mind, which is a direct result of self-satisfaction in knowing you did your best to become the best that you are capable of becoming." He also believed that no person was better than the structural foundation it was built upon. By this he meant you can't be in peak condition without the others around you also being in peak condition. The strength of the organization is more about healthy individuals and healthy communication between the individuals than the lines across a chart.

As a leader, I focus on the scope of responsibility of my team members, not on the tasks alone. I focus on the individual people in my organization and their strengths, weaknesses, and potential, rather than on some dotted lines that add more stress and confusion rather than clarification. People know who's in charge. They all know who the boss is. But if you rely on a chart to inspire your team members and give them the confidence to do their jobs well, you are often making their roles more confusing. If you work with your team to ensure that all members understand their individual responsibilities and how they can do their jobs better, you won't need an organizational chart.

Many people are able to rattle off the fifteen blocks of the Pyramid. The foundation consists of

Industriousness and **Enthusiasm** with **Friendship, Cooperation,** and **Loyalty** making up the rest of the foundation. **Self-Control, Intentness, Alertness,** and **Initiative** make up the second tier while **Condition, Team Spirit,** and **Skill** are at the heart of the Pyramid. The above qualities may help someone develop **Poise** and **Confidence,** and a person who possesses all of those qualities may achieve **Competitive Greatness.**

One of the incredible things about the Pyramid is that it applies to individual success as well as a team or organization's pursuit of peace of mind. Everyone brings different skills to the work and organization. As we create teams and bring different skills and talents together, someone needs to fill each of these roles for the group to achieve success.

Some of the often overlooked and underrated parts of John Wooden's Pyramid of Success are the other qualities that hold the blocks together. The blocks represent a series of necessary traits that help develop and maintain the qualities of the Pyramid. Wooden calls these ten traits the "Mortar" of the Pyramid. Mortar is what holds together any structure, and without it, even the strongest materials could fall apart. We should all concentrate on working on these traits to solidify the work we do on developing the blocks of the Pyramid.

These critical traits are needed to tie everything together to create the ultimate definition of success. Those nine qualities are:

- **Ambition:** Can be a huge asset if focused but a huge detriment if out of focus.
- **Adaptability:** Being able to meet the challenge of different situations and to work well with others.
- **Fight:** Not giving up and being prepared to endure tough battles.
- **Faith:** Believing in your objectives and in yourself.
- **Patience:** Knowing the road will be tough and not expecting too much too soon.
- **Integrity:** Being pure in your intention and doing what you say you are going to do.
- **Reliability:** Others knowing they can count on you, which creates respect.
- **Honesty:** Being truthful in both your thoughts and your actions.
- **Sincerity:** Being genuine will help you build and maintain relationships.

An organizational chart is often about winning. Do you want your team members spending their time and energy figuring out how to climb your chart and "win" for themselves? Or do you want them to be focused on getting the job done and to cooperate with each other to achieve corporate rather than individual goals? Consider throwing away the chart and thinking more about how you can foster real communication across your entire organization that is focused not on winning, but on making things work for your customers.

CHAPTER 8

My Team

*"Great achievement is usually born
of great sacrifice, and is never
the result of selfishness."*

—Napoleon Hill

I believe leaders are readers. So I'm usually reading at least three books simultaneously about leadership, sports, politics, or culture. I'm enamored of leadership theory and practice, and I love to read about leaders who bootstrapped themselves and overcame great obstacles. One of the topics I've read a lot about is teamwork. I love it also because I was a college athlete and am still a sports enthusiast today. A quote I have hanging on my wall is from Bill Bradley, former Princeton basketball star and United States senator:

> *A team championship exposes the limits of self-reliance, selfishness and irresponsibility. One man alone can't make it happen; in fact, the contrary is true: a single man can prevent it from happening. The success of the group assures the success of the individual, but not the other way around.*

Teamwork is simply how people work together cooperatively and collaboratively to get things done. Managing a team is hard work, and even the best leaders are challenged by it. There's not one single way that works best, as every team and every situation is different. So you have to stay nimble and be sensitive to your surroundings and the individuals on the team.

I've learned a lot along the way, including something I've become quite strident about, and that's how to describe teams.

Most of the teamwork content I've read and the teamwork consultants and gurus I've studied often refer to the phrase "my team." Many of my colleagues, usually executives, also often use the phrase "my team" when referring to the people in their organizations. They will say something like, "My team is doing a great job" or "My team needs to work harder to meet goals." Calling the people in your organization "my team" is a huge mistake, and it often defeats the entire purpose of building effective teamwork.

Fundamentally, it's not your team. The people who work for you are not "your" anything. They don't belong to you, nor do they belong to your company or organization. They are individuals who have lives outside of work. They each have a job title and responsibilities at work, but they do not belong to the organization. I'm not the CEO, either. I happen to fill the position of CEO in my organization. It's a role. None of us *is* the role we hold at work. Each of us is doing a job, and it's usually just for a limited time, after which we will move on and serve in another role. But we're never the role itself. The role of CEO is not mine, and the organization is not mine. I'm Patrick, not CEO. The people who work with me are Jennifer,

Charles, Andrea, Maria, or Brandi. Nobody has the right to call them "mine."

It might look and feel like an insignificant difference in terminology, but great leaders are authentic people, and they inspire with truth and honesty. When you refer to the group of individuals you supervise or oversee as "my team," you are implying possessiveness over them, even ownership. It makes the team about you and not them.

I don't want to skip over this too fast. I believe the use—and in the business world, the overuse—of the term "my" undermines everything we are trying to do in leadership. Even when followed by profuse praise and talking about how great they are, using that type of term brings it back to being about you. None of us likes to work for someone who makes all of our work about him.

A cohesive team is rarely built on the back of a single individual. Let's think about how athletic coaches refer to teams. You rarely hear a coach say, "My team played great today" or "My team put up a real fight." They will often refer to the team as "the team" or "our team." They also focus on the individual. I like how Nick Saban describes teams and teamwork. He says, "Individuals make the team. How they think and what they do is important to the team. It's important who these people are."

73

The definition of teamwork is the absence of selfishness, right? That much is obvious. Selflessness cannot be achieved if you're constantly reminding everyone that the team belongs to you. Imagine if you tried to motivate your team with these words: "OK, everyone, we can get more done today if nobody here worries about who gets the credit. So I want my team to be selfless and not think about which one of my team members is going to get the credit. You're my team, and my team works together under me to get a job done. Let's go!" Clearly you wouldn't win the team over with those words! But that's exactly what you sound like when you call the team "my team."

It also implies they have no choice in the matter. When you imply ownership over individuals, you're subconsciously telling them that they have to do the work. It's mandatory because "you are mine" and a part of "my team," so "do what I say." But, in fact, nobody has to do anything. The members of the team don't have work for you, and they can quit tomorrow. They don't have to fill the roles they currently serve in. They don't have to listen to you or do what you say. All team members are there voluntarily, unless maybe they are a part of the Armed Forces, and even then, there are certainly elements of their roles and jobs that are voluntary.

So how do we do this in a positive way?

First, I have to admit, this is a hard habit to break. It is such a natural way to approach the conversation. As I've tried to be very thoughtful about this, I try to use such terms as:

- Our team
- The team
- Our organization
- Specific names when possible, so I'm acknowledging individuals

The words we use matter. While using "my" is such a universal word choice in leadership and management, it to be a real hindrance to success. It centers you, the leader, as the most important part, when really we want our teams to get the credit.

CHAPTER 9

Be Curious

*"Curiosity will conquer fear even more
than bravery will."*

—*James Stephens*

I've spent the vast majority of my career working in nonprofit organizations in management and fundraising roles. As I began to dig deeper personally and focus on the recovery process, I felt strongly that my career needed to stay in the same sector. I needed to build a component of my future around helping people. I had further realized the structural differences in our society that picks winners and losers, and I wanted to do my part to influence it for more equity.

A fundraising maxim I learned early in my career is: "Ask for money, get advice; ask for advice, get money." No, this is not stolen from the Pitbull song, "Ask for money. And get advice. Ask for advice, get money twice," but frankly Pitbull also understood the idea as well! What does this mean in the context of being curious?

The basic premise is that to truly engage with people—and in the case of fundraising, that is ask them to donate money—you have to be curious. You have to be more *interested in them* than you are *interesting to them*. Did you get that? You need to remove yourself from the center of attention. It's not about you. If you're going to get someone's genuine attention and engage with them in a very real and personal way, you have to focus on their needs, not on your own needs. You have to become a genuinely curious person.

Curiosity is relevant for all business leaders, not just those of us in the nonprofit world. And it's not just a ploy or a game to get what you need. Curiosity literally expands your empathy. When you're curious about others and talk to people about themselves— about their challenges, their struggles, and even their successes and triumphs—you begin to take on their persona and understand *how* they feel, to see things from their point of view, and to imagine yourself in their shoes. This is the beginning and root of all real relationships. Even scientists agree that curiosity helps strengthen relationships. One recent study asked strangers to pose and answer personal questions, a process scientists call "reciprocal self-disclosure." They found that people are literally rated as warmer, more attractive, and less anxious if they show real curiosity in the exchange. These same scientists created the Curiosity and Exploration Inventory (CEI), which demonstrated that curious people are happier. Why? Curious people are like magnets.

This goes without saying, doesn't it? Imagine yourself on a date. How attractive are you if you drone on and on about yourself? What are your chances of a second date, a third date, or eventually a wedding if you don't take genuine interest in your significant other?

The same holds true in all relationships, especially in your business relationships.

In 1868, in the United Kingdom, Benjamin Disraeli and William Gladstone were competing for the position of prime minister. Both were well-known leaders and brilliant people, but they had very contrasting styles and personalities. The difference between the two men, however, was summed up by a woman who had dinner with both Disraeli and Gladstone a week before the election.

The lady both men dined with was Jennie Jerome, Winston Churchill's mother. When a journalist asked Jerome about her impression of the two men, she responded: "When I left the dining room after sitting next to Gladstone, I thought he was the cleverest man in England. But when I sat next to Disraeli, I left feeling that I was the cleverest woman."

Disraeli spent the whole evening asking her questions and listening intently to her responses. He wanted to know everything about her, and he tried to steer the conversation toward her. Naturally, she talked, and we always feel good talking about ourselves.

Not surprisingly, Disraeli, the person who mastered the art of making other people feel important, won the election.

So how do you become a more curious person? For starters, I've developed questions that I pose to the people in my life on a regular basis. I've found that after asking someone one or all of these questions, my relationship with that person begins to grow by leaps and bounds. We go from acquaintance, vendor, donor, or business associate to friend. Moving someone into the friend box is not only a good thing for business goals, but you'll also soon find yourself with a bunch of friends. And friends make us better people, less anxious, and less lonely!

Here are three kick-off questions I like to pose when I meet someone:

CAN YOU TELL ME MORE ABOUT THAT?

This is an open-ended question that literally lets the other person take the conversation where *he* wants to take it. You're asking him to tell you his story. Of course, he can tell you. In fact, he's probably desperate to find someone, anyone, who's willing to listen to his story. Once he begins to tell you more, encourage him to keep going. You might be surprised at how quickly the person will open up to you, even about very personal matters. Why? Few people are willing to ask and then listen without reciprocating with advice or even judgment. So when you ask someone to tell you more, just listen. You won't gain anything by trying to tell him what to do. In fact, if you do try to provide advice, he may regret answering your question.

WHY DO YOU THINK THAT'S TRUE?

This question begs not merely for facts, but opinions. When you ask someone *why* he thinks or feels the way he does, get ready, because he may express a perspective that you don't agree with. But that's not the point. When you ask someone to freely offer his own perspective, and you respond with respect, then he'll truly enter into a real relationship with you. I find that these days, especially, people practically expect confrontation when offering their opinions. As a result, they build self-protecting walls all around themselves and will not find real solutions to their problems. I tear down these walls by asking, listening, and respecting.

WHAT COULD BE DONE TO CHANGE THINGS?

Now you're not only asking the person to share his story with you and to tell you why he feels the way he does, but also what he would do about it. What do you think is the solution? If you were in charge, what would you do? I've discovered that this can be a loaded question, but it's also one that people are most desperate to talk about. We all have some strong ideas as to what we'd do if we were in charge, right? I bet you think about this every day. We all do. But few people are willing to listen, and hardly anyone asks the question. When is the last time someone asked you this question? When the people around you know that you're open enough to listen, you're well on your way to becoming not just their friend, but a confidant.

I have found that the higher you go in an organization, the more impactful this curiosity can become. I've recently had the opportunity to be interviewed by grad students doing a research project involving an exploratory conversation about a partnership. These conversations have been focused on information from my work with Vibrant Health or from one of my colleagues. After I answered all of their questions, I made a point of stopping them before they wrapped up the call to ask about them: "Tell me about your role. What is your background in relation to this work?" You might be surprised how people react to this, especially when they don't expect someone to have time or interest. I can assure you that it changes how they feel about the conversation when they wrap up their day.

THE ABILENE PARADOX

The questions above help build relationships with team members that open the door for them to provide ongoing feedback and idea sharing. That open door is critical to avoiding the "Abilene Paradox."

The Abilene Paradox is a short book written by Jerry Harvey in which he takes on the challenge of managing agreement. In a nutshell, here is a paraphrase of the relevant story:

A few decades ago, a family was sitting on the porch playing dominoes and drinking lemonade on a very hot Sunday afternoon in Coleman, Texas. This family consisted of a mom and dad and their son and his wife. It was 104 degrees, and they had no air conditioning in their house.

At some point in the afternoon, the dad suggested that they get in the car and drive to Abilene to have a meal at the cafeteria. They all agreed that the trip was a pretty good idea. So they got into Dad's Buick, also with no air conditioning, and drove fifty-three miles to Abilene. They had dinner at the cafeteria and got back into the sweltering car and drove the fifty-three miles back home.

After they had been sitting on the porch with another glass of lemonade and had taken up their dominoes game again, the mom said, "You know, I really did not want to go to Abilene. The car was hot, the food was crummy, and it took a long time."

The son chimed in, "I didn't want to go, either. Why did we do that?"

And the daughter-in-law said, "I sure didn't want to go."

And then the dad said, "Well, I really did not want to go; actually, I was just making conversation."

So they had spent three hours getting to Abilene and back on a hot day to eat bad food because none of them said, "Wait a minute, I don't want to do that. I don't think that is a good idea."

This behavior happens all the time to both individuals and organizations. They go where they don't want to go. They do what they don't really want to do. They become something they never intended to become. They end up in Abilene because nobody just stops and says, "Hang on a minute; I'm not sure about this."

CHAPTER 10

Focus on Well-Being

*"If you want to lift yourself up,
lift up someone else."*

—Booker T. Washington

The physical and mental well-being of your team is as important as your sales quotas, your conversion rates, and your quarterly earnings. I'm not always taken seriously when I say this, but it's true. We as business leaders need to stop fooling ourselves into believing that our staff members can leave their problems at home. They can't and they don't.

I'm the CEO of a healthcare organization, so I see up close and personal what you may see only from afar, or you may never see at all. I see the consequences of poverty, neglect, violence, trauma, and the associated toxic stress that literally changes how the brain develops and affects how the body responds to stress. I see firsthand how what happens during early childhood can have detrimental effects on both short-term and long-term outcomes for learning, behavior, mental and physical health. The effects of trauma are initially processed by the developing brain, but the cascading consequences are expressed in many ways later in life. All of this plays out not only at home, but also in the workplace. And don't fool yourself into thinking that it's rare for individual staff members to suffer from poor well-being. If you were to spend a day with me in my office, I'd show you otherwise. In fact,

I think you'd be stunned to discover that *most* of your staff suffers to some degree.

What's more, work and home are intertwined today in ways that were unthinkable even a decade ago. Digital communication is now a constant flow, not only between coworkers, but also between family members and friends before, *during*, and after work. Some employees are now working remotely full-time or part-time, further complicating how their personal lives affect their work. Many are even working from home full-time. So the idea of compartmentalizing home from work might sound appealing, but the reality is much messier than that. As anyone who has ever received a call at work from his child's school knows, the barrier between professional and domestic life is more like a door than a wall. The emotional traffic that moves through that door can lead to positive effects in the other, and vice versa. Rather than pretending that we live in a world with a clean separation between work and play, it's more productive to acknowledge reality: Life is complicated, and the anxiety can be sky high. And it's hitting your bottom line.

While it may not be your job to literally provide your staff with a mental or physical diagnosis or treatment plans, you do have to be attuned to the fact that when our systems are stressed and overworked, our ability to problem solve, make good and rational decisions, and process information decreases, leading to poor job performance. And we all know what poor job performance leads to: unhealthy and unprofitable organizations that don't grow. If you choose to ignore an individual's well-being, you also choose to ignore the well-being of your entire organization. To be an effective CEO in America today, you have to find ways to recognize and address well-being.

Again, as the CEO or head of your organization, you aren't a medical professional. You certainly can't take on and treat trauma or attempt to resolve or heal brokenness. But you can build a workplace that helps to mitigate or lessen the pain, particularly during work hours. This can't be a sidebar or after-thought. We all need to be intentional and strategic about the well-being of our staff.

How can you positively affect the well-being of your team members? There are many ways to organize an approach that helps give team members physical and mental breaks during the day. Offerings such as yoga, meditation, or other organized mindfulness techniques are helpful. Even a short walk can be a recharge. When you allow people to mentally unwind, you're helping them to regroup internally. It also goes without saying that CEOs need to provide their staff with reliable health insurance programs. A sick staff is no good to anyone, and we possess a moral obligation to our workers to provide them with the ability to get healthy.

The biggest thing here isn't the specifics of what you offer at your workplace or what you do. That will likely be unique for each person on the team. Most important is that you make the space for it to be OK to not be OK. This is the leader's job. You do this sometimes by acknowledging when you aren't in the right space mentally. You don't have to be perfect. Your willingness to acknowledge it, own it, and work on it gives the space for others to do their own work without fear of judgment or criticism.

We often have conversations at our workplace that may start with something like "I'm not in a great headspace on this issue and feeling pretty defensive, so that may be clouding my judgment…"

This type of comment does a few things. First, it protects you. It may seem counterintuitive, but it's true. It gives you the buffer to say what you are thinking or feeling with an initial disclaimer about what may be influencing that reaction. This isn't a free pass to say whatever you want, but it does create some freedom to express a potentially challenging opinion. Second, it gives people space to give you feedback. By saying, "Here is how I'm feeling on this personally," it opens the door that you are willing to hear another perspective. Lastly, it gives people power in their own work to acknowledge when they are having a hard time.

Also, and this may seem small, but take time to check in with your team. The art of the check-in is something I've spent a lot of time developing as a way to build relationships and to provide emotional support, particularly when I become aware that someone is going through a tough time. Of course, people have different preferences about how they connect with each other at work. While some people may want to sit and talk, some may prefer a digital chat and others may not be open to engaging at all. But learning *how* to engage with employees in a way that they feel comfortable is the key to creating a sense of community. Try to seize the small opportunities to connect. Establish connections with your colleagues that communicate that you value, understand, and care about them. Be present, be curious without bias, and seize small daily opportunities to connect authentically. For example, a simple *"How are you doing?"* or *"How can I support you?"* goes a long way with nearly everyone.

I'm not afraid to speak from a position of vulnerability, which I believe people appreciate and trust. I was not always a person with strong, positive well-being. You know from the words you've read in this book that there was a time in my life that was challenged mentally, physically, and emotionally. So when I check in with my team members, I'm not afraid to bare my own soul and remind them that I, too, once sat in a cell, feeling very much alone and broken. I think this gives others the strength to push forward, to confront and accept their own difficulties, and to work on their own well-being.

CHAPTER 11

Don't Avoid These Three Words

"I always entertain the notion that I'm wrong, or that I'll have to revise my opinion. Most of the time that feels good; sometimes it really hurts and is embarrassing."

—Anthony Bourdain

At some point, everyone has struggled to say these three words. However, the smartest people I know aren't afraid to say them. It is a very simple statement, really:

"I don't know."

It is a simple statement, but it can be so hard to say, particularly in front of coworkers or the boss. We have all worked with people who refuse to say they don't know the answer. The problem is, when someone consistently refuses to acknowledge something they might not know, nothing they say can be trusted. Often people would rather make up an answer, guess, or outright lie than admit needing to do some research to get the right information.

As tough as it is to say these words, there are several benefits to saying, "I don't know."

BUILDS TRUST

Nothing builds trust like honesty. It sounds so simple, but we often screw it up. People get caught up thinking, "If I always have an answer, if I'm confident, or if I'm in the know, they will trust me." It's not that complicated. Saying, "I don't know, but I can find the answer and get back to you" does far more to build trust.

AVOIDS PROMISES YOU CAN'T KEEP

An often used cliché is "Under promise and over deliver"—and again, it is a cliché because it's true. One way to do that is to avoid making too strong a statement, particularly about something you cannot fully control. I recently had someone on my team at work telling me:

"If we do this, it will change this outcome by X%."
"Do you know that for sure?" I asked.
"No."
"Do you believe it will work?"
"Sure."

Opening this conversation with "I don't know for sure, but our research shows doing this will change the outcome by X%" leaves an opening to be wrong. You aren't making promises you can't keep.

SHOWS STRENGTH

We hold ourselves to a high standard. We don't want to show weakness. We are scared of being vulnerable. But admitting we don't have the answer isn't either of those things. It shows strength to admit a gap or a blind spot. It is comfort in your ability and your intellect that you don't have to know everything to still be talented and smart.

PROMOTES DISCUSSION

No one likes to work with people who have all the answers. It can be exhausting. The reality is that none of us can do it alone. A willingness to acknowledge that we don't know something encourages engagement with those around us. Often, the people we work with can fill in some gaps. They have insights and knowledge that we don't. The exchange of information and ideas is empowering, and it encourages people to do more.

SHOWS WISDOM

Knowing what you don't know is often as important as knowing what you do know. When people willingly admit a lack of knowledge on a given topic, it tells me they have a high level of self awareness and have considered their strengths and weaknesses. They know where they have gaps and rely on others to help fill those gaps.

STRENGTHENS OTHER OPINIONS

Everyone seems to have an opinion. Often people have strong opinions on things they actually know very little about—just look at Facebook on any random day. Being open about what you don't know gives much more credibility to the opinions and knowledge you do have.

Saying "I don't know" is simply part of developing honest relationships with your coworkers. Effective work relationships must be built on honesty. Along the way, admitting you don't know everything can result in the benefits listed above. It's too bad this phrase is so rarely used. As Socrates put it, "The only true wisdom is in knowing you know nothing."

CHAPTER 12

Give before You Take

*"Leadership is not defined by the exercise
of power but by the capacity to increase
the sense of power among those led.
The most essential work of the leader is
to create more leaders."*

—Mary Parker Follett

The first rule of influence and getting things done is reciprocity.

Robert Cialdini has written several books on influence and persuasion, and he is an expert in the field. His first principle of persuasion states that human beings are wired to return favors and to pay back debts. We generally try to treat others as they've treated us.

For example, the last time you visited a restaurant, there's a good chance that the waiter or waitress treated you extra special. He or she probably smiled a lot, may have told you a joke, or possibly even complimented you in some way. If so, did you feel obliged to give the server a better tip? Of course you did! That's the law of reciprocity.

You can also see how this principle plays out in many ways in an office environment, in a company culture, or even in partnerships between two companies. As my career has progressed, I can't tell you how many times I have seen this relatively basic principle work both for and against people. Sometimes it comes back to bite when it's violated.

I try to keep this at the forefront of my mind during the workday. It's not always easy. The problem is that we often approach meetings, email communication, or even conversations around the office coffee pot focused on what *we need*. We talk about the funding *we need*, the actions *we want* from the team, or the end goal *we are trying to accomplish*. We're self-centered in our approach to problems. This is backwards, though. You're less likely to get what you need when you start with yourself and your own needs. It violates the law of reciprocity.

I'm not suggesting that you shouldn't have your own needs in mind. After all, in business and in our personal lives, we all have goals and objectives we need to accomplish. But the issue at hand is the end result and the outcome. What's the best way to get there? Rather than being focused on ourselves and our own needs, we should instead start with what we can do to help others. We should ask ourselves such questions as "How can I give back?" and "What value can I bring to the other person?" Start with other people's needs in mind, not your own. When you do that, the law of reciprocity kicks in.

While many relationships have the reciprocity component built in, such as in a marriage, it can't be transactional. Relationships have to be authentic. You can't approach this with a mindset of "I'm going to give this, and that is what I want to get." In most successful relationships, there is openness and some flexibility as the relationship is built over time to identify what is wanted in return. All good relationships include a healthy dose of the law of reciprocity. Be empathetic and be real.

This isn't a new idea. Benjamin Franklin wrote in his autobiography: "He that has once done you a kindness will be more ready to do you another, than he whom you yourself have obliged." This has come to be known as the Benjamin Franklin Effect, a cognitive bias that causes you to like someone more after you do that person a favor, especially if you previously disliked that person or felt neutral toward him. For example, the Benjamin Franklin Effect could cause someone who disliked you to start liking you after he does you a small favor, such as loaning you a book or helping you with an assignment. Your view of another person elevates in your eyes simply by doing something for him. Give it a try. You'll be surprised at how the relationship begins to improve.

Research proves how the law of reciprocity helps us become better leaders. In Adam Grant's bestselling book, *Give and Take*, he shares how our individual reciprocity styles impact our success (or lack thereof).

According to conventional wisdom, highly successful people have three things in common: motivation, ability, and opportunity. If we want to succeed, we need a combination of hard work, talent, and luck. Yet there is a fourth ingredient, one that's critical but often neglected. Success depends heavily on how we approach our interactions with other people. Every time we interact with another person at work, we have a choice to make. Do we try to claim as much value as we can, or do we contribute value without worrying about what we receive in return?

Grant describes three reciprocity styles (how we interact with other people): Givers, Takers, and Matchers. These styles include every type of interaction and where our focus is on the outcomes we are looking for. His research was to uncover which of these styles is the most successful.

It might be logical to assume Takers are the most successful, but the research showed something else. Givers ranked at the very top and at the very bottom. Matchers and Takers filled out the middle. But how could Givers be on both ends? What's the difference between the most successful and least?

Grant's research found that successful Givers aren't just more other-oriented than their peers, but they are also more self-interested. They value the greater good, and they also value their own interests and needs. They are altruistic and ambitious, and the ability to put themselves on their own priority list is what prevents them from getting steamrolled, burnt out, and left behind.

The answer is less about raw talent or aptitude and more about the strategies Givers use and the choices they make. We all have goals for our own individual achievements, and it turns out that successful Givers are every bit as ambitious as Takers and Matchers. They simply have a different way of pursuing their goals.

Givers approach their interactions as win-win. They don't gain when someone else loses; they want to see everyone win, and if they can bring people along with them, all the better.

Givers, Takers, and Matchers all can—and do—achieve success. But there's something distinctive that happens when Givers succeed: it spreads and cascades. When a Taker wins, someone else usually loses. Research shows that people tend to envy successful Takers and look for ways to knock them down a notch. In contrast, when Givers win, people are rooting for them and supporting them rather than gunning for them. Givers succeed in a way that creates a ripple effect, enhancing the success of the people around them. You'll see that the difference lies in how a Giver's success creates value instead of just claiming it.

CHAPTER 13

People Watch Your Reaction

"Leadership is a series of behaviors rather than a role for heroes."

—Margaret Wheatley

I try to look at all the life around me to help me do a better job at work. Work is just a subset of life, and we can learn important lessons outside of work that help us on the inside. Sometimes even my own children teach me important lessons.

As a father, I've learned how my children often look at me, and I mean directly with eye-to-eye contact, when they are in a crisis situation. They're unconsciously monitoring my response to their crisis. For example, when my toddler daughter falls down and hurts herself, she will immediately look at me as she decides how critical her situation is. If she sees that I'm cool, calm, and collected, she gets herself together and soon displays the same coolness. If she sees me panic, even a little bit, she goes into a full throttle freak-out mode. Her reaction is based partly, sometimes mostly, on my reaction. Her pain is tied directly to mine.

If you're a parent, you've also learned this lesson, and you've learned to try extra hard not to show any anxiety until or unless it's absolutely necessary. Sometimes it's hard, right? When you see your child take a bad fall, your mind might start to drift toward the Emergency Room as you watch the fall. But you don't show it. Instead, you pick him up, brush him off, smile, and even try to make him giggle. "You're

OK," you say as you hug and reassure him. Your child can see the calm look in your eyes, and he grows more confident in the crisis.

Let me give you another example of how people unconsciously recognize your reaction. Let's say you're engrossed in a task, maybe reading a book, when suddenly you have the creepy feeling that someone is staring at you. It's like a sixth sense, probably an adaptation that literally kept our ancestors alive. You've experienced this, right? The biological phenomenon is known as "gaze detection," and neurological studies suggest that a complex neural network is at work inside your brain. We don't know the mechanism that makes it work, but in fact, we all know when someone is staring at us. Think about it: Just looking at someone is a social cue. You don't even have to say anything before another person recognizes your response to something. We're constantly scanning the horizon to view how and what other people are thinking.

This is important to realize and keep at the forefront of your mind: All the people in your life, at home and at work, are looking for your reaction to every situation. If you're a leader at work, everyone who works for you and with you is using your reaction to base their own feelings and emotions. Have you ever considered treating them just like you treat your own children?

Our workplaces are filled with anxiety, stress, and conflict, just like the rest of life. People take hard falls at work every day. This should come as no surprise, and I've learned to expect that buttons will be pushed and drama will abound in the workplace. We especially see it during tight deadlines, when we don't get something we want, or when a customer flies off the handle.

So what should we do when conflict or hurt feelings erupt at work? We should react the same as we do with our own children when they're hurt. When you see conflict or pain at work, you can choose to react or respond. There's a big difference.

A reaction is instant. It's driven by biases and prejudices in your unconscious mind, backed by years of negative experiences. When you say or do something "without thinking," that's the unconscious mind working in the moment without taking into consideration other people's feelings. It's all about you, not other people, and we often regret those reactions later.

A response, on the other hand, usually comes more slowly, not knee-jerk. It's based on information from both the conscious and unconscious mind, and it takes other people's feelings into consideration. Responses are rarely regretted because they align with our core values.

I vividly recall a predicament when a colleague was marching down the hall spewing expletives after a disappointing meeting with his boss. An ongoing issue boiled over, and he just lost it. The commotion left the rest of the team uncomfortable, and they too got angry. His reaction became their reaction, and soon the entire team became dysfunctional. As leaders, when we react in such a manner, we are being impulsive, shortsighted, and usually not giving much thought to what we are doing. Imagine if you did this with your own child.

By responding, rather than reacting, we create space away from the negative emotions surrounding the crisis. It gives us the opportunity to be more patient, act with more humility, build more logic (and less emotion) into our approach, and be more self-aware. Think about how much self-awareness you force yourself to display with your own children. You intentionally exhibit calm even in situations that might need to trigger a more anxious response. You do this because you know they're looking for it.

In a communication exchange at work, things can easily escalate when the other person also reacts without thinking first, turning a conversation into a heated argument. If you learn how to respond and not react, people will do the same. People don't like stress and anxiety. They prefer calm, but they sometimes need another person to help keep them calm.

So how do you respond when other people are unsure how to respond?

First, be patient. It's not always easy, but when we use this virtue to our advantage to assess a situation and get a better perspective, we think more rationally and make better decisions. I've always said that patience is not the ability to wait, but it is the ability to keep a good attitude while waiting. Believe me, there are times when I'm ready to explode, and before my experience in jail, I did explode frequently. I was definitely not the kind of person other people would look to for calm.

But I've learned how to be patient with myself and with others. I'm self-aware enough to now understand that all the people around me are looking to me before they decide about their own demeanor and emotional response.

Second, try to avoid the temptation of reacting from your bruised ego. When you react out of pride, you get in your own way. You can't even see the solution, as you're too busy looking for a way to make yourself the winner. So instead of using sarcastic comebacks or put downs, draw from your own inner strength, trusting in the moment to a different, better outcome. Humility is the ability to give up your pride and still retain your dignity. It's concerned with *what* is right, not *who* is right. Patience combined with humility is a powerful combination that gives you and everyone around you the strength to work things out for the betterment of everyone.

Finally, work on your self-awareness. It really wasn't until I was in solitary confinement that I finally found myself. When I was utterly alone, I had the time to see myself for who I really was. It was a crucial time for me to begin to focus on how my actions, thoughts, and emotions aligned or did not align with my personal beliefs. As I became more self-aware, I could better evaluate and manage my emotions. Put simply, I could better interpret other people's actions, feelings, and thoughts more objectively. I could look at the whole picture and find more compassionate responses.

The emotional intelligence guru, Daniel Goleman, once wrote, "If your emotional abilities aren't in hand, if you don't have self-awareness, if you are not able to manage your distressing emotions, if you can't have empathy and have effective relationships, then no matter how smart you are, you are not going to get very far."

The next time someone flies off the handle, or the next time you're confronted with a problem or crisis, here's a way to positively blow that person away with your response. Be patient, act with humility, and practice self-awareness. What comes next may surprise you. Suddenly, you're the leader in the room. Suddenly, everyone around you will be attracted to you like a magnet. You'll find yourself in the enviable position of the person in the room everyone wants to be. It literally gives you more power in a situation. To react otherwise gives you less power and control. Leaders understand that everyone around them is constantly assessing their reaction and response.

CHAPTER 14

Own Your Mistakes

"Not everything that is faced can be changed, but nothing can be changed until it is faced."

—James Baldwin

One of my most profound experiences in jail was an awareness that came from the similarities in the conversations I had. Not one person I met described himself as a criminal. Not one. One group was screwed over by the system, another group was innocent, and then finally, one group was made up of victims of circumstance. But nobody was a criminal—at least in his own mind. But in reality, we all were.

But this was a revelation for me in how I thought about engaging with people. I had done some awful things. I was surrounded by people who had done awful things (allegedly). But no one was viewing himself, in that moment, as being defined by that awful thing. Similarly, the people we work with aren't defined by their worst, or frankly their best, moments.

You are not your worst decision, your worst action, or the worst thing you ever said to anyone. But it's interesting how often we choose to define ourselves by our worst mistakes. We take the darkest parts of our lives and draw a lot of conclusions about ourselves. We are embarrassed about them, and we sometimes keep them a secret, often living in fear that someday we'll be "outed."

Most of us don't operate that way with anyone else, though. We don't think about our spouse, our parents, other loved ones, or even our friends that way. We don't focus on their worst attributes or mistakes, even those who are closest to us whom we know a lot about. When we think of them, we accept and see their mistakes by the light of their circumstances. We often recognize that they did the best they could with what they knew in a difficult situation. But not so for ourselves. We beat ourselves up over it.

I want to confront you about your own life and past mistakes, as I did in my own life. I want to offer you a different way of thinking about them and dealing with how they affect your life today and your future.

I was sitting in my basement on January 26, 2020, when the notifications started on my phone that Kobe Bryant and his daughter had died in a helicopter crash. I was stunned. Rarely does a death announcement of someone I've never met have a significant impact on me. But this one did. I wasn't always a Kobe fan. In general, I appreciated him more as he got older and wasn't at his best. That appreciation only grew as he retired and stayed out of the limelight. Also, being a dad of three daughters and coaching two of them in basketball, I could relate to and respect his involvement in his own daughters' lives.

Like many of us, Kobe wasn't perfect. He had a very high-profile sexual assault case against him. I can understand why some people reacted negatively to the outpouring of love and support for Kobe after his death. I can understand that, for some, what he was accused of is a stain forever on him as a person. I'm not going to attempt to change anyone's mind on that or to condone what happened.

I think, given his stardom and excellence on the basketball court, a couple of things were overlooked in how he tried to learn from his mistakes. A lesser known story from Kobe was his transition on LGBTQ issues. In 2011, he was fined $100,000 for using an anti-gay slur toward an official. He was called out for it. His initial apology was as weak as most celebrity apologies, but following that, he put in the work. He reached out to members of the LGBTQ community and advocacy organizations. He became a vocal ally for the LGBTQ community. He used his fame, resources, and reach to spread positive messages and to change minds.

Kobe was a complicated individual, and you can't separate the good from the bad. Like all of us, he was all of those things.

You've read in this book that I was an alcoholic and an addict, and that I spent time in jail. I made some huge mistakes. I could make a lot of assumptions about myself based on those mistakes, and at first I did. When I walked out of jail, I certainly wasn't proud of what had just happened to me. It wasn't the kind of thing I wanted to put out there in conversations with friends or family, and certainly not with strangers. Was I embarrassed? Certainly. Did I regret my actions? Indeed. Did I let it hold me back? Not for long.

Not long after I left jail, I was driving down the road and passed an area in my community that has long been an encampment for homeless people. As I passed, a man crossed the street heading into the encampment, and I recognized him. I had met him when I was in jail. It hit me that I had just been living with him. We both made a bad decision and wore the same orange jumpsuit, we ate the same bad food together, and we both lay there staring at the same cement ceiling. We were leading vastly different lives at that moment but also not far removed from either of us being in the other's spot. This was a critical juncture for me. It was at this point that I became determined not to replicate my old life ever again, and also that my mistakes were not going to define me or hold me back. To some degree, the homeless man and I probably had vastly different life experiences, and I certainly was born with more privilege, but notwithstanding, I was not going to let my worst mistakes control the rest of my life. I wasn't going to return to the encampment that had ruined my life.

Not long into my sobriety, I was called by a headhunter about a job opportunity. I openly shared my story about my felony DUI conviction and asked her to keep it confidential until I could share it on my own. Though she agreed to do so, she didn't stick to her word. Later, when confronted, she bluntly told me, "You're only one hundred days sober. Who is to say if that is actually going to last?" First, let me just say that is an awful thing to say to someone in recovery. But for me personally, that has served as a significant motivator and has cemented an approach in how I think about sharing my story.

So what did I do?

I knew that I couldn't change anything about my past and how I once behaved. History is history. There was nothing I could do to erase it. So I decided to be open and honest about it. Even more, I decided it could be used as a strength. I felt that if I owned it, it couldn't be used against me, either in a malicious way or by accident.

I stopped attending Alcoholic Anonymous (AA) because it too was controlling. This is not to say that AA is a bad thing. For many people, it's helpful, or even critical, during their recovery process. But for me, I couldn't thrive until I freed myself from my past and got my life back. Nothing was going to control me, and I took an extreme approach to being open and honest about my mistakes. I stopped hiding it and made it very public. I owned it all in a way that nobody could ever use against me. I decided the only way to control my predicament was to take control away from everyone and everything else. I decided to own it.

There is a movie scene that I think is a great analogy for this change in ownership. If you have seen the movie *8 Mile*, starring Eminem, this may come to mind immediately. If you haven't, here are the basics. Eminem's character, B-Rabbit, is in a rap battle with his archrivals. For anyone new to this, a rap battle is a freestyle tournament where competitors aim to criticize and belittle their opponents. The rapper with the best lines and criticisms wins. In the final battle, B-Rabbit opens his time with a long list of all the negative things he expects his opponent to say about him. He lists every embarrassing thing that could be said about his life and closes with "Now tell these people something they don't know about me." He turns the table entirely, and his opponent is speechless and essentially quits.

Our mistakes can be treated the same way. Ownership and transparency related to what has happened can have an incredible impact.

When I was in the final stages of interviewing for my current role with the search committee (made up of several members of the board of directors), I took the very open, upfront position of being honest about my mistakes. I didn't wait for any questions. In fact,

I made it a part of my presentation. I told them the entire story from beginning to end and owned every embarrassing part of the story. I asked them to judge me more on my reaction and response than to judge me on the event itself. I'd like to think that the board members respected my honesty on that day, and that they told themselves, "If he's that honest with us about this stuff, he'll be honest with us about business challenges, too."

Being honest about your mistakes isn't just a good approach for those of us who have made a mistake big enough to land us in jail. It's a good policy for each and every mistake you make. Don't ever try to cover up or blame others for what went wrong. If you messed up, admit it and own it. It doesn't have to be a big deal. In fact, if you simply acknowledge your responsibility and move on, it probably won't be a big deal. Insecure leaders fear looking weak and run from their mistakes. They think it makes them look worse and that it will cost them respect. On the contrary, I believe that in leadership, vulnerability is the ultimate strength.

In the *Harvard Business Review*, leadership gurus Richard Farson and Ralph Keyes write about the "failure-tolerant leader." They studied how leaders at America's most successful companies and organizations deal with mistakes. Interestingly, their approach is similar to what I discovered. They confronted their own errors publicly, and they encouraged their team members to do the same. "Far from revealing weakness," they write, "admitting mistakes shows a leader's self-confidence. It helps forge closer ties with employees and colleagues. A blunder admitted is empathy earned. Leaders who don't cover up their errors reveal themselves as human—they become people whom others can admire and identify with."

CHAPTER 15

Fundamental Attribution Error

"Never attribute to malice that which can be adequately explained by neglect."

—*Napoleon Bonaparte*

I referenced this earlier, but as I sat around a jail room talking, I discovered that no one there views himself as a criminal. There are many reasons people credit with why they end up sitting in a cell. Often they acknowledge making a mistake—but making a mistake and belonging in that place aren't always the same thing.

But the other component is that no one wants to view himself as a criminal. From an outsider's perspective, it is easy to judge people on their worst decisions, but that isn't how those of us sharing a meal in jail viewed ourselves. We judged ourselves based on our intentions, which were not evil or criminal, and not based on our actions. We thought about those decisions as situationally bad but not criminal.

While everyone in that jail had an excuse, the irony is that we didn't even believe each other's stories. Everyone outside of jail thinks everyone inside is guilty, and everyone in jail also thinks everyone in jail is guilty—except himself! We also like to think we'd *never make* the same bad decisions. The problem for me was that I was in jail, and there wasn't a damn thing I could do to explain away my actions. My actions put me in jail, not my intentions. I knew I was there for good reason. I didn't like it, and I admittedly didn't think I deserved it, but I knew I wasn't innocent. But it took me a few days in solitary confinement for me to confront myself in this way.

This is one the most important lessons I learned in jail, and I'm so glad I did because it's made me a better leader.

I learned that our general reaction to other people's mistakes and errors is almost always based entirely on their actions. We don't give people the benefit of the doubt. We don't cut them much slack. We hold them 100 percent accountable for their actions, no matter what else is going on in their lives. Yet we make all sorts of excuses for our own actions!

This happens to all of us all the time. I actually think this tendency in human nature is one of the biggest problems in work relationships. I see it practically every day. If you show up late to a meeting, you cut yourself all sorts of slack: it was traffic, the dog, or the line at Starbucks. But if someone else, someone who reports to you, shows up late for a meeting, well, that's a different story. You immediately, at least internally, blame that person for being late. It doesn't matter how bad traffic was; you literally think the other person should have taken that into account. "Excuse me, but can you please do a better job of managing your calendar!"

This lack of empathy actually has scientific origins. The phrase "fundamental attribution error" was coined by psychologist Lee Ross after a paper he published in 1977. In his now legendary research, Ross explained that we tend to explain someone's behavior based on internal factors, such as his personality, while we underestimate the influence of external factors, such as the neighborhood he grew up in. For example, we might believe someone else is unemployed because he is lazy. But when we lose our own job, we tend to think it was our employer's fault. Of course, there are times when we're correct about our assumptions, but the fundamental attribution error is our tendency to explain the behavior of others based on their character and not on things they can't control.

Why do we so readily blame other people but find ways to not blame ourselves? I believe one reason is that we are more familiar with our circumstances. If we are laid off from our job and become homeless, we know that the poverty we find ourselves in is not the result of our character, but the result of our circumstance. But when we see another person who is homeless, we see only the end result, and we make an assumption about what led to it. I also think we simply don't want to see ourselves in a negative light. Have you ever met anyone who shared with you that he views himself as stupid or ugly? Of course not. We all want to see ourselves in a positive way.

So how do you see yourself? Do you unconsciously practice fundamental attribution errors? If you're like most people, when it's pointed out to you, you suddenly realize you do a lot more of this than you realize.

I encourage you to begin to embrace more grace in the workplace. Grace isn't a word we often use when describing workplace behavior. But when we think and talk about how to build better workplace environments, it's important to remember that we all need a little unmerited favor. None of us deserves to be fully responsible for our dumb mistakes. We simply don't deserve it, and none of us can live up to the expectations we put on each other.

In his best seller *7 Habits of Highly Effective People*, Stephen Covey encourages us to "Seek first to understand then be understood." We spend a lot of time in conversations preparing our own response or thinking of what witty comment we will have in return. As Covey says, "We are filled with our own rightness, our own autobiography. We want to be understood. Our conversations become collective monologues, and we never really understand what's going on inside the other human being."

CHAPTER 16

Good Leaders Are Good Followers

"Courage is what it takes to stand up and speak; courage is also what it takes to sit down and listen."

—*Winston Churchill*

Even when you're in charge, sometimes it is still your role to get the coffee.

One of the most important traits of good leaders is they are really good followers. If you can't follow, you'll never lead. I think it's ironic that we don't read books about "how to be a good follower." We read a lot about how to be a good leader, but never about how to be a good follower. When was the last time you went to a Followership Seminar? I think leading and following are very much intertwined, and too often leaders forget how to follow.

What's a good follower? Good followers are:

- Committed to the mission
- Constantly learning
- Hardworking
- Loyal

Being a good follower is an important part of how people get themselves into positions of leadership, right? We all know that and experience it in our work. But then once we're promoted into a position of leadership, we sometimes turn the follower part of our brains off. We get so consumed with being a good leader, we think we're the resident expert of all things and people. This attitude can really end up hurting both the leader and the organization.

I'm the CEO of a healthcare provider. We take care of nearly 20,000 patients per year, and I'm not a clinician. I am in no way qualified to make all of the necessary decisions to operate our organization. Ideally, I can ask informed questions and provide additional thinking to decisions, but without a doubt, many times the best thing for me to do is keep my mouth shut and follow the lead of those best trained and experienced to make those decisions.

Admittedly, this can be really difficult, particularly when expertise isn't as clear cut as, "Are you a doctor?" What might happen if I tried to blindly lead in these situations? It could very easily become a disaster!

I'm sure that you too find yourself in situations where you feel the need to lead. Your job title and role demand leadership so you try (too hard) to lead and forget to follow. I always say that leaders aren't as smart as they think they are. Just because you're a leader does not mean that you're the smartest one in the room. Our job as leaders should be to find and then follow the people who are smarter than we are.

COVID-19 brought about many great examples of this. I know a number of organizations and companies that never planned to have physicians involved in their leadership teams, either through consulting or through employing them full time, but the pandemic forced us into that position. Even in healthcare, where physician leadership is everywhere, the pandemic forced physicians to lead in areas where they had not previously been asked to be the decision makers.

I think this is a way that really great leaders shine.

So how does a good leader remain a good follower?

KNOW WHAT YOU DON'T KNOW

To make room for others at the top, you have to share the spotlight. That means both internally and externally. To make this possible, you really need to do some self-evaluation. Do you know what you don't know? Do you know what your weaknesses are? Do you know where others excel in places that you are challenged? Or frankly, do you know tasks that people thrive on that you can't stand to do?

These are all questions you should be thinking about and maybe even asking others for input. The team members around you will see things you can't see, both good and bad. You should be asking them for input at least regularly enough that you are aware of opportunities.

CHECK YOUR EGO

Let others shine. While this seems easy, it can often be difficult for leaders to take the low road, especially during a public presentation. I saw this up close and personal during a key public presentation during the COVID-19 pandemic here in Kansas City.

A month or so into the pandemic, the University of Kansas Health System (UKHS) launched a Daily Morning Media Update in which they discussed the latest COVID data and other topics that surrounded the pandemic. This was a 30-minute program targeted at the media and was streamed online. It turned out to be a brilliant media strategy as the content shared was used for stories by all the local television stations, and it connected the health system to the community in much deeper ways.

But one thing that was distinct about the program was UKHS's CEO, Bob Page, who was not publicly a part of the presentation. He let others take the lead on the program, including Dr. Steven Stites, executive vice president and chief medical officer, and Dr. Dana Hawkinson, director of infection prevention and control. Bob is an incredible leader. He, along with Tammy Peterman, the Kansas City market president, led a remarkable turnaround of this institution, due in part to how they shared the spotlight with other important members of the UKHS team.

It might seem obvious for medical professionals to be hosting a program focused on pandemic response and safety, but it is not often that leaders allow others to be out front. The nuance here is that some leaders will get all of the information from the expert on the team, even allowing that expert to decide what happens, but the announcement of facetime comes from the leader. This is a huge miss!

GET THE COFFEE

I somewhat mean this as a metaphor, but not entirely. Sometimes the best thing you can do as a leader is the small, mundane task. It doesn't mean you aren't the leader if you bring coffee and donuts into the morning meeting. Sometimes leadership means doing smaller tasks that need to be done so that other people can get their jobs done.

For example, we once hired a new human resources director who convinced me that some of the administrative tasks that our chief medical officer and I were doing would be better handled by an executive assistant. It would help to free up our time. I pushed back against this suggestion previously because I felt the organization wasn't big enough yet. I didn't want to give up managing my calendar or other similar tasks that an executive assistant might handle for me. But I eventually caved in, and I soon saw the tremendous difference it made in my ability to get more work done.

Later that year, we had an important compliance review to compare our operations to federal requirements. The executive assistant coordinated the review and was a big part of researching our internal operational processes. Ahead of the final meeting, I asked if the team wanted donuts and coffee from our local coffee shop. I knew that everyone had put in a lot of work and it would be a long day. Although I was involved and certainly central to the day's presentation, I wasn't central to the final details or the meeting itself. So I took charge of the coffee and donuts. Our executive assistant stopped me to say that in all of her years, she had never had her boss get her coffee. "I've always been the one to get the donuts!" she told me. In *that particular moment,* not only was this the right thing for my skill set, but it also sent a powerful message of appreciation to the team.

Most of the time in our roles as leaders, we need to be out front, leading, making decisions, and coordinating communication. We usually do have to lead. But we can't forget the times when we must follow the lead of others. It can be so easy to fall into the trap of thinking that we are responsible for all of the decisions. The truth, though, is that we aren't responsible for all of the *decisions*; we are responsible for the *outcomes*.

CHAPTER 17

Winners Want the Ball

*"There's nothing truly to be afraid of,
when you think about it, because I've failed
before, and I woke up the next morning,
and I'm OK."*

—Kobe Bean Bryant

I'm generally not one to remember quotes from motion pictures, but one particular quote stuck with me from the 2001 sports movie *The Replacements*, starring Gene Hackman. It speaks directly to leadership, specifically the kind of leader we should aspire to be.

If you don't remember the movie, or if you haven't seen it, *The Replacements* is the comedic story of a professional football team during a players' strike. The movie is loosely based on the 1987 NFL strike, and specifically the Washington Redskins, who won all three replacement games without any of their regular players and went on to win Super Bowl XXII. In the film, though, all the players are "has beens" or other players who failed to ever make a team's roster. It's like the adult football version of the famous movie, *The Bad News Bears*.

As you might imagine, the story covers the challenges of washed-up football players who either are being thrown back into the spotlight or who are now in the spotlight for the very first time. The physical, mental, and emotional struggles the players face are challenging, and how they ultimately overcome their individual and team challenges to win in the end is very inspiring. Of course, they are coached by Gene Hackman. Who else would you choose than the guy who took little Milan High School to the Indiana State High School Basketball Championship?

The plot surrounds the interim head coach Jimmy McGinty, who chooses Shane Falco, a former NCAA All-American whose career went to pieces after a lopsided Super Bowl loss, to be his quarterback. Falco lives in a houseboat and makes a living doing hull maintenance on private yachts. He initially refuses, but McGinty persuades him, believing that Falco can still become the player he was meant to be.

At the end of the first game, the score is close and the replacement players have an opportunity to score the winning touchdown. There's just enough time for one last play. The last play of the game will determine a win or a disappointing loss. Coach McGinty calls in the play, but at the line of scrimmage, Falco calls an audible to turn the play into a run. The play fails in a disastrous fashion.

Afterwards, back on the sideline, Coach McGinty and Falco have this tense verbal exchange:

Jimmy McGinty: Falco! If I had wanted Cochran to have the ball, I would've called it that way!

Shane Falco: I read blitz.

Jimmy McGinty: Bullshit! I put the game in your hands, and you got scared.

Shane Falco: I READ BLITZ.

Jimmy McGinty: Winners always want the ball when the game is on the line.

To me, the exchange isn't exactly what you think. You probably think McGinty is saying that winners like to win. Winners like to be, and need to be, the center of attention. I'm sure there are different ways to interpret it, but I don't think this is all about wanting the ball at crunch time. I interpret McGinty's response as a willingness to accept the outcome of the play *no matter what that outcome is*. It's more about sacrifice than it is about winning. McGinty is telling Falco that he's not willing to lose.

We all know leaders who are so confident that they are always taking matters into their own hands. They always see themselves as "victors" and "saviors." They love the limelight and the feeling they get when they shine in front of their team. In sports, we sometimes call these people "ball hogs." They love being in the spotlight. And nobody likes a ball hog, even if and when they do succeed.

To me, wanting the ball at the one-yard line should be about leading and not winning. Leaders should be willing to take "the hit," no matter the resolution. This is really powerful for teams to see from leaders, both their colleagues and their bosses. As leaders, it is our responsibility to recognize those situations where we need to make the tough decisions, take the tough meetings, and take the tough phone calls, whether we're going to win or lose. It's not about winning or losing. It's about taking responsibility.

True leaders take responsibility for EVERYTHING. They turn each misstep into an opportunity to learn. Instead of pointing fingers, they turn inward and find solutions. When you lead a group of people, they become reflections of yourself, and when leaders pass the credit and take the blame, the team ends up winning.

Acknowledgments

This book doesn't happen without Chesney (my wife) being the supporter and rock that she is. She is the backbone of our family, the consistent encourager and believer in me. She always has my back.

My daughters Avery, Makenna, Lowen and Myla Jett. While the chaos of our house isn't conducive to a project like this, they are my inspiration and greatest joy in life.

For the last 40+ years, my parents David and Mary have been giving me leadership lessons. Both worked in higher education, ending with my father retiring after 17 years as the President of William Jewell College. Together they have helped shape my approach to leadership and a deeper understanding of people.

Nearly six years ago the Vibrant Health board took a chance on me. They overlooked my personal history and the fact I had never been a CEO before. The entire time I have been in this role they have given me nothing but support. They provide room to grow and learn and explore while also trusting in my leadership ability and where we are going as an organization.

Thank you to Andrea Thomas Ramsey, Polly Thomas, Mindy McDermott, Mike Heckman and Tracy Lockton for your leadership in chairing our board over the last six years. Your mentorship and friendship has empowered us to accomplish many amazing goals!

I'm incredibly lucky to work with a leadership team that is passionate about our work and committed to building an amazing organization that improve the health of our community. And probably most importantly, they put up with me.

A huge thanks to Tom Freiling and Freiling Publishing for the opportunity and partnership to produce this book.

It is said you are the sum of the company you keep. I hope that is true because I am blessed with some amazing friends:

Thank you Mayra Aguirre for your friendship and willingness to give me candid and open feedback and advice. Not just on this project but on the work we are to accomplish at Vibrant Health you are a relatable motivator and believer that all things are possible.

In the last year I've had an amazing opportunity to participate in the Helzberg Entrepreneurship Mentoring Program and have learned a tremendous amount from my mentor Bruce Reed. Your ability to see the challenges we are working through clearly and help develop a plan to keep work through them has been a tremendous asset to me personally as well as Vibrant Health.

One of the critical things that has helped me over the years is a group of people from various backgrounds and experiences that are willing to share their perspective on a range of issues from personal to professional.

Thank you to this group for always taking my call and being so incredibly supportive.

9 781956 267754